T4-BBV-714

sketch by Bill Werthman

YESTERDAY'S NEWS

Nix Wadden

Library and Archives Canada Cataloguing in Publication

Wadden, Nix
   Yesterday's news / Nix Wadden.

ISBN 978-0-9809369-7-1

1. Wadden, Nix. 2. Reporters and reporting--Newfoundland and Labrador--Biography. 3. Newfoundland and Labrador--Biography. I. Title.

PN4913.W33A3 2008   070.92   C2008-905743-0

Cover Design and book layout by Diane Burke Lynch

Cover photo: A.N.D. (Anglo Newfoundland and Development Company) logger interviewed by VOCM's Nix Wadden at Victoria Lake January 1959

Back cover photo: Newfoundland Press Club members attending a presentation to Past President Art Pratt: (left to right): Harold Horwood, Steve Herder, Harvey Clark, Noel Vinnicombe, Mark Ronayne, Gerry Freeman, John Puddester, Arthur Pratt, David Gilbert, Arch Sullivan, Gerry Bowering, Nix Wadden, Mel James, Bill Werthman and Don Morris

Printed and Published in Canada 2008

~ DRC Publishing ~

3 Parliament Street
St. John's, Newfoundland and Labrador A1A 2Y6

Telephone: (709) 726-0960
E-mail: staceypj@nfld.com

YESTERDAY'S NEWS

Radio and TV Reporting
in the Smallwood Era

by

Nix Wadden

Whimsical recollections of events, issues and personalities covered working in St. John's news media in the 1950s and 60s

Highlight Events

- Smallwood Government at its Apex
- Diefenbaker Election Wins
- VOCM-CJON Rivalry
- IWA Strike
- Term 29 Controversy
- PC Party Struggles
- Jamieson Doing the News

Personality Glimpses

- Omar Blondahl
- Edsel Bonnell
- Harry Brown
- W.J. Browne
- Bill Callahan
- Richard Cashin
- Dalton Camp
- Bob Cole
- Denys Ferry
- Maurice Finn
- Harold Horwood
- Don Jamieson
- Max Keeping
- Bob Lockhart
- Jim McGrath
- Bob Moss
- John Nolan
- Gerry Ottenheimer
- George Perlin
- Art Pratt
- Ed Roberts
- Mark Ronayne
- Bill Squires
- Grace Sparkes
- Arch Sullivan
- Tony Thomas
- Bill Werthman
- Sylvia Wigh
- Bruce Woodland

CONTENTS

FOREWORD

A lot has been written about pre-Confederation Newfoundland, but less about the couple of decades that followed the rancorous 1949 decision. Even less has been written about the 1950's and 60's from a journalist's point of view. Nix Wadden's memoir is a vibrant account of the heyday of home-grown media in Newfoundland and Labrador, a time when radio stations, magazines and newspapers seemed to crop up everywhere, nurtured by an enthusiastic and nationalistic press corps. Besides covering history in the making, the author made history himself when, in 1953, he became the first reporter hired by VOCM, one of this province's most popular radio stations. His first job at VOCM didn't last long, but when he returned four years later, he had a lot more journalistic experience and was able to help the station become a more professional news gatherer.

I grew up knowing the author as my "Uncle Ron," my father's younger brother. His first name, Ronald, is used only in the family, but most people know him as "Nix", a contraction of his second name, Nicholas. He and my aunt Madeline moved to Ottawa in 1966 when I was just ten years old. He was better known to me for the generous packages he and my aunt sent our family each Christmas, rather than for his career as a journalist. It's a rare privilege for a niece to be given so much insight into a favourite uncle's early life, and even more so, to be asked to introduce his memoir. I am happy to report, with a clear conscience, that you don't have to be related to him to enjoy this book or learn a great deal from its pages.

Nix Wadden, the new province, and broadcasting in Newfoundland and Labrador, came of age at pretty much the same time. His job as a radio reporter gave him a front row seat at many of the political developments that shaped Canada's newest province as it tried to ease into its new citizenship. As a sideline, he participated in the backroom work of the Progressive Conservative party, vainly trying to rally enough opposition to unseat Joey Smallwood's powerful Liberal machine. Lucky for us all, he kept a thorough archive of clippings and his own radio scripts, which prove to be a rich repository for his lively storytelling. His voice in this book is replete with the wit and candour for which he's well known to friends and family.

There are a lot of gems here; some political mysteries solved, and plenty of new fodder for trivia buffs. We now have eyewitness proof that the legendary photographic memory of broadcaster, and former federal Cabinet minister, Don Jamieson, was not an urban myth. My uncle wrote copy for Jamieson, who anchored "News Cavalcade", a popular television program of the period. He tells us that Jamieson had only to glance through the copy briefly before performing it live on air, almost verbatim, without aid of a teleprompter or the written page.

Yesterday's News is social history at its best. My uncle purchased his first car in 1955 for a mere $1,364.75. It came in handy when he took a second job covering sports for the Evening Telegram. Nix spent a lot of time inside the newly constructed Memorial stadium, built by the citizens of St. John's to honour their war dead. There's a vivid description of the 1955 Valentine's day hockey match, between St. Bon's and the Buchans Miners, that will make readers nostalgic for the strong local hockey tradition that used to exist in this province; the kind of hockey that makes spectators feel a close kinship to the players, and a stronger stake in the game's outcome. St. Bon's won a thrilling victory, made all the sweeter because the Buchans Miners had imported semi-professional players from the mainland.

The description in this book of the Newfoundland loggers' strike of 1959 is riveting and one of the most extensive I have read, told by someone with a ringside view. His account of the divisive Term 29 issue, one of the first federal-provincial rifts to arise after Newfoundland and Labrador became part of confederation, will resonate strongly now because of the ongoing conflict between Premier Danny Williams and Prime Minister Stephen Harper. Provincial Tories felt as deeply betrayed by a Conservative Prime Minister in the 1950's as many do today. Premier Danny Williams might welcome the rebirth of the United Newfoundland Party, a political party that some disenchanted Tories created to oppose Prime Minister John Diefenbaker!

My uncle wore two caps during his broadcast career but was to learn that they didn't match up too well. Hidden under his reporter's cap, Nix spent some time as an executive member of the provincial Progressive Conservative party. Conflicts between the two callings arose from time to time, ultimately forcing him to choose between his political work and his career as a journalist. Journalism won out, as eventually he gave up his active involvement in the Conservative party.

This memoir arrives at a time when Newfoundland and Labrador is celebrating a robust 87 years of radio broadcasting. In 1921, Newfoundland's first radio station began as VOS, operated by J.J. Collins, a local representative of the Marconi company. By 1924, seven of the remote mission stations, operated by the International Grenfell Association, were equipped with radio sets, and by 1931 St. Anthony had its own station, VOR, operated by the charity. Bell Island had its own radio station that same year too, but not surprising, the greatest radio activity was taking place in St. John's, where there were already four stations operating by 1924. The Dominion Broadcasting Company, a subsidiary of the Avalon Telephone Company Limited, opened a 5,000 watt station in St. John's in 1932. The station was called VONF - the "Voice of Newfoundland". It was "640" on the AM dial, where CBC radio in St. John's can be found today. (The Canadian Broadcasting Corporation took over VONF after confederation). A news bulletin, sponsored by the prominent Newfoundland merchant, Gerald S. Doyle, was first broadcast on VONF in 1932, and before long, became an important part of the province's social fabric. The story of radio in Newfoundland and Labrador, with its long list of colourful characters, merits a book of its own. *Yesterday's News* whets our appetites for more.

Newfoundland's first successful commercial radio station, VOCM, was founded in 1936 by Joseph L. Butler, but relied for its news programming on a service, similar to VONF's Doyle News Bulletin, that was provided by Harvey and Company, its main commercial sponsor. Working with Harvey's News, my uncle was largely responsible for the transfer of its operations to found VOCM's own news service, with him in charge, in 1957.

Nix writes with gratitude about the mentors and colleagues who helped him along the way, and his book is truly a "who's who" of journalism in this province in the middle of the twentieth century, including accounts of the early careers of such luminaries as broadcasters Bob Cole and Harry Brown.

My choice to enter journalism in 1977 was not a conscious effort to follow my uncle's footsteps; more likely it was influenced by my father's love of newspapers that were dutifully clipped everyday and stored away to satisfy his hobby as an amateur historian. However, I'm beginning to suspect I got my first job in journalism because of my uncle's connections. He worked as a proof reader for *The Daily News* in 1952. Twenty years later, I landed a summer job doing the very same thing, for the same newspaper. When I was hired to work for CBC television in the summer of 1977, I found myself working beside some of my uncle's former colleagues. They always referred to him warmly and with great respect. He and I both seem to have played bit parts in the first six decades of post-Confederation broadcasting in Newfoundland and Labrador.

My uncle has always been generous and supportive to his nieces and nephews. It's not surprising then that I would feel closer to him after reading his memoir. What unconscious impact did he make on me when, in 1971, he took me to lunch at the National Press Club while I was on a school trip to Ottawa? I must have absorbed some of his love for the profession from encounters like that.

I confess to having had some reservations before agreeing to write this Foreword. What if I didn't like the book? How could I recommend it to other readers in any objective way? Those fears were quickly laid to rest as I began to read. Within these pages you will meet a man who has remembered, and written down, some very important details about life in St. John's in the 1950's and 1960's, and whose own life story should be reassuring to anyone at loose ends about starting a career. Nix Wadden's foray into journalism, you'll learn, was anything but predetermined. This memoir is also a valuable reminder of the tremendous privilege journalists enjoy, with our close up view of social history in the making. It's a job that comes with a great deal of responsibility. My uncle exercises that responsibility by writing down all that he has learned during his news career, and passing it on to another generation.

by Marie Wadden

1

Beginnings

FINDING THE WAY

Getting into the wacky and wondrous world of journalism was far from my mind when the doorway to Memorial University College opened for me one fine September morning in 1947. Truth to tell, my powers of concentration on anything academic were less than lively as body aches and blisters lingered from a long and arduous weekend walk. I was recovering as best I could from a hastily decided entry in the annual Daily News Ten Mile Walk.

Going to Memorial was in fact another rashly conceived decision, except that entry into the realm of higher learning had been for me a foregone conclusion. I took it for granted once the June Grade Eleven exam results assured me of junior matriculation with honours. My only faux pas, and a big one it proved to be, was the hasty and totally illogical selection of college faculty I had signed for - engineering. A bonehead choice for one totally inept in matters technical - spurred only by desperation for lack of any obvious career goal, and the fact that engineering was that term's flavour of the month. No fewer than 45 first year engineering students were enrolled that fall - out of a total student body of merely 317. The error of my ways came home to me as I floundered in efforts to comprehend the mysteries of physics and chemistry, so I shifted my attention to pursuits of far more interest - mainly sports, and girls. Year one of academe was, in short, a total dud. Small consolation it was to note than only 11 of those 45 engineering 1st year's completed the 3rd year.

A major distraction in that formative year 1947-48 was the great debate on Newfoundland's political future and the highly charged campaigns for a return to Responsible Government, entry into Confederation with Canada or a hybrid third option, Economic Union with the United States. Keenly interested in this issue, as was just about everyone in Newfoundland, I got a chance to play a minor but exciting part as it reached its climax.

THE 1948 REFERENDUM

My first paying job was a one-day stint as a poll clerk in the June 3, 1948, referendum in which Newfoundlanders were asked to choose their future form of government. Fifteen years earlier, self-government status as a British colony had been surrendered in favour of government by commission, a body appointed by the British government. This resulted from financial bankruptcy brought on by repercussions from the Great Depression of 1929.

World War II, for all its dreadful consequences, brought sufficient prosperity to Newfoundland to prompt calls for restoration of self-government. By 1946, Britain under the newly elected Labour government convened an elected National Convention to determine Newfoundland's future course. After many months of bitter debate, dominated by demands to consider confederation with Canada, a majority of convention delegates recommended the resumption of "responsible government." The British government, however, spurred by a massive public petition mounted by confederation advocates, decided to offer a referendum choice of three options.

Vividly do I remember the day when an excited education student burst from the phone booth into the Memorial University College common room to shout "Confederation (he pronounced it CON-federation) is on the ballot paper!" And thus the voting options were among continuing Commission of Government, restoring Responsible Government, or accepting Confederation with Canada. From that day on, campaigning and deep-seated emotional controversy swept throughout the land, polarizing the entire populace as never before. Though too young to have a vote myself - voting age was 21 - I fervently supported the Responsible Government cause but, unlike some of my friends, had not gotten involved in the anti-confederation campaign.

My poll clerk duties in the June 1948 referendum involved assisting the returning officer who conducted referendum voting at St. Clare's Mercy Hospital in St. John's. A significant locale for me, as that's where

I was born nearly 18 years before. Toting ballot forms and ballot box from room to room, it was pretty exciting to hear all the patients' chatter and feel the suspenseful atmosphere as they went about marking their X's. A few made no bones about how they were voting, but most kept their own counsel.

When ballots were all counted, the June referendum failed to deliver a clear cut decision. Of 155,777 votes cast, Responsible Government led with 69,400 votes, Confederation got 64,066 and Commission of Government trailed with 22,311. Deeming this outcome insufficient, authorities called for a second and final referendum with just two choices - Responsible government versus Confederation - to be held six weeks later on July 22, 1948.

My modest insider view of the political process continued at the Second Referendum as I was hired as so-called election clerk, assisting the appointed Returning Officer for St. John's West District. Getting the six week job, thanks entirely to my Dad's acquaintance with the incumbent, Joe FitzGibbon, I found him a most engaging character. As Irish as paddy's pig, as my Dad would say, he knew everybody, called all men "brother", and had no trouble lining up polling stations and clerks and accessories needed for the big day. A constant pipe smoker, he was continually digging into his pipe with a pocket knife, cleaning out dregs of tobacco and scattering much of it all over the place. An auctioneer by trade, he spoke to everyone, in person or on the phone, as if he were conducting a public sale, without benefit of a microphone. While eccentric, he had a heart of gold and was clearly in his element, arranging polling stations and enlisting helpers to ensure smooth running of the referendum vote.

Our office was in the Colonial Building, site of the Newfoundland House of Assembly before Commission of Government, and destined to be home to the Province of Newfoundland House of Assembly for about ten years after confederation. I heard many stories of the old days, including the great riot of 1932 when angry citizens stormed the building in a violent protest against the government of then Prime Minister Sir Richard Squires.

Swearing in referendum staff was a daily routine in which I played my clerical part, but had its moments of unconscious humour. I was amazed how many clerks solemnly swore to perform all of the duties required of them as poll clerks in the "electrical district" of St. John's West.

When ballots were finally counted, St. John's West and other urban districts, plus such areas as the southern shore, stood firm for responsible government, but the charms of confederation swept most of the rest of the island. Final count: Confederation 78,323, Responsible Government, 71,334. The die was cast.

Attending Memorial University College that fall, I limited my political activities to attending a few public rallies, and lamenting the relentless march toward union with Canada. I did take part in a passionate responsible government rally at the CLB armoury one night in December. When the meeting ended, I marched with hundreds of others toward the gates of Government House to protest to Governor Gordon MacDonald against Britain's acceptance of the narrow confederation majority. But to no avail.

Governor MacDonald, a gruff teetotalling Welshman appointed by the British Labour Government, was widely despised by the anti-confederate majority in St. John's. His reputation as a partisan proponent of confederation despite his supposedly neutral status earned for him undying scorn. And a certain immortality as commemorated in this fervent farewell tribute published March 8, 1949 in the columns of the Evening Telegram, a dedicated confederation supporter, on the eve of his departure for England:

A FAREWELL

The prayers of countless thousands sent
Heavenwards to appeal thy safe return
Ennobled as thou art with duty well performed
Bringing peace, security and joy
Among the peoples of the New Found Land.
So saddened and depressed until your presence
Taught us to discern and help decide what's best for
All of whom fortune had not smiled
Remember if you will the kindness and the love
Devotion and the rest that we people have for thee -
Farewell.

Chagrined Telegram owners frantically pulled in as many copies of that edition as they could when someone noticed that the first letter of each line spelled out "THE BASTARD". As John Crosbie noted in a recent memoir by veteran St. John's photographer Frank Kennedy, MacDonald was heartily disliked, not only for his partisan support for confederation, but also for his fervid opposition to drinking and card playing.

In his book, Flashes From the Past, published in 2,000, Frank Kennedy revealed, for the first time that I know of, the authorship of that famous Farewell "tribute". Confirmed by the estimable Grace Sparkes, the cleverly crafted shaft of satire was composed by a formidable trio of ardent responsible government advocates - barristers John G. "Jack" Higgins and Robert S. "Bob" Furlong (later to become Chief Justice of Nfld.), and Grace herself.

A bittersweet consolation nonetheless.

MONTREAL CALL BOY

Confession time: I was once a Montreal call boy.

No, not what you're thinking, not at all. Let me explain. It was in the hot and humid summer of 1952, and I was in Montreal, doing odd jobs - very odd jobs - for the Canadian Pacific Railway (CPR). It was a sort of summer job. Certainly one of the most unsatisfying I've ever suffered, but it put a few cents in my pocket during a very lean period. Maybe working for CPR was inevitable. Back at St. Francis Xavier University, which I had just put behind me, we had a fellow student fondly known to everyone as "Choo Choo" Liston. He earned that moniker honestly, constantly spouting reams of factual data about railways in general, CPR in particular, and the schedules and timetables of any rail line one could mention.

Hired on as a casual, available to do whatever tacky odd jobs needed to be done, my call boy chores were simple enough. I had to tramp along a maze of railway tracks in one of those giant railway yards, in the middle of the night, to call and wake up locomotive engineers and firemen who were due to take trains out in an hour's time. I was, in short, the wake-up man. Or boy, rather, and boy, was I unpopular. Those hard-boiled railwaymen were dead beat from long hours and long hauls, too tired to take kindly to a scrawny cheeked kid banging on their door and beseeching them to get out of bed at 4 a.m. Dodging boots tossed by surly sleepers proved an indispensable survival skill on those early summer mornings.

Somewhat of a comedown from the lofty halls of learning I'd left behind me. Ending of a final term of study at St. F.X. in Antigonish, N.S. had been less than glorious, trailing a cloud of uncertainty for lack of requisite degree credits. Flight to Montreal was an unplanned reaction, achieved only by hitchhiking with a bulky suitcase as sole companion. Ominous in part, as a friendly Quebec City driver, Montreal bound to see his "friend girl", fell victim to a less than cautious American road jockey who crushed in his rear fender. Not staying to offer any witness statement, I hopped in another vehicle for the last lap, arriving in front of Windsor Station.

I found a home away from home in a McGill University fraternity house, 3421 Drummond St., off Sherbrooke. Board was cheap and the frat folk were friendly but I had to find work real soon. I came with precious little cash in hand and no known family in the area. I scanned scores of newspaper help wanted ads at the Bibliothèque de Montréal, entranced by the overwhelming demand for short order cooks. None at all for former students steeped in 18th century English literature and a smattering of book taught French. Someone I met suggested that CPR hired summer casuals, so I knocked on the right door and got in.

Somehow, dredged from a trunk full of tattered old files my packrat compunctions have managed to preserve, I've retrieved a messily typed record of my month or so of hard labour in the corridors and outposts of CPR's Montreal domain. June 2 - day 1 of my brief railroading career - found me at St. Luc, 8-4, in the role of checker. My tasks were to note down the variety of railway cars included in each train unit - e.g. boxes (box cars), baggage, mail, flats, reefers (refrigerator cars), tanks (tank cars), passengers (though seldom were they found in the railway yard), and cabooses. Next day, same place, same hours, same duties. Day 3, same place but midnight to 8 a.m. and duties: call boy.

Day 4 was my first doing by far the messiest and most demeaning of chores handed to me anywhere, identified simply as "carbons." Locale was Place Viger, hours were 8 to 5, but the duties consisted, solely and continuously, of extracting from piles of office stationery multiple sheets of carbon paper used to produce copies in those far off pre-xerox times. The hideous blue black carbon ink soiled fingers and shirtsleeves and anything they touched, and the smell lingered far into the evening. Those were not among my finest hours. Day 5 returned me to the carbons centre but, thankfully, for a half day only.

A hoped for benefit of enduring these thankless duties was the opportunity to practise some French conversation with my mainly French colleagues. Fresh from a succession of French language and literature courses, I fancied myself fairly knowledgeable with a passable accent but alas, my efforts to embark on French dialogue proved utterly fruitless. As soon as I started, others answered calmly in faultless English. One fellow, who took a friendly interest, turned out to be obsessed with pumping me about English words and grammar, and constantly answered me in English, so I soon gave it up. Maybe it's just excessive politeness on their part but francophone Quebeckers, of that era at least, never gave willing anglos a chance to build on their bilingual best intentions. Quel dommage!

My second week with CPR was probably the worst of them all as in midweek I ran completely out of money, and payday was yet to come. My job assignment for that week was to be a station assistant at Adirondack Junction, an important junction with the New York Central

Railway in the south western suburbs of Montreal. It was a long bus ride - something like eight miles - taking me over the Mercier Bridge. Monday went fine and I returned Tuesday morning, but heading back to my frat house room at 5 p.m. closing time posed a small problem. I didn't have bus fare. Nothing for it then but to start out to walk. And walk I did, hour after hour, staring into drainage ditches along the way in hopes of finding a loose dollar or even a dime. Not even a miserable penny! Arriving home about 10 p.m., footsore and feeling extremely sorry for myself, I dined morosely on bread and milk.

Next morning, still penniless, I phoned in to beg off sick, and wondered what to do. Moping around my room didn't help, so I wandered about nearby streets, stopping in for somewhere to sit down at the mammoth Montreal railway station. Staring at the hordes of passengers coming and going, I suddenly spotted a familiar face. Doug Haynes, a fellow student of mine a few years earlier at Memorial University in Newfoundland, was en route to Petawawa for summer army training in ROTC, and had most of the day to kill. I borrowed a few dollars from him, and we went off for the day to quaff a few beers in nearby taverns, exchanging stories and wishful fantasies about the alluring ladies we saw around us. A student chaplain though he claimed to be, my benefactor for the day had an ever ready eye for feminine charms.

Restored by this unexpected bit of luck, I nevertheless needed to resort to desperate measures next day to earn bus fare to let me return to my post at Adirondack Junction. Sheepish and shame-faced, I skulked into a pawn shop and walked out with $6 for my gilt-surfaced X ring, proud emblem of my yet unearned St. F.X. university graduation. A star crossed symbol, I retrieved it from the pawn shop after payday, only to lose it forever many years later in a house break-in. I miss it - it was always good for a lukewarm laugh for its usefulness in place of a genuine signature.

Assignments for the rest of the month followed similar routines - checker, call boy, carbons, with an occasional break as shed messenger. In late July, my duties were sometimes required at a location that proved a little more interesting. This was the huge Angus shops where scores of train combinations were sorted, using an elevated hump structure by which individual cars were channelled to appropriate tracks by simple law of gravity power. Checking the type of cars in each set could be trickier here as there were so many lines of track to traverse without falling victim to all of this power in motion.

My fraternity house haven was spacious enough for me to try tapping away at a rinky dink portable typewriter, introducing me to a self-learned, crude but relatively adequate ability to type. Grinding out occasional letters home to family and friends set me up, so it seems, for a lifetime bound to a keyboard. My typing style for years remained a mite unorthodox - a three finger exercise using two fingers on my right hand and one on my left.

Communicating thus with the outside world probably helped, so that by mid summer, I was ready to make a move. Surely, the charms of Montreal life had faded fast under the burden of too little money and too little food - and the occasional plea for financial help from the home front proved too much of an embarrassment. So I headed at last for home, and an end to a memorable, but all too forgettable, railroading career.

Compensation for carrying out these invaluable services in aid of Canada's pioneer railway was modest by any standard. A cherished keepsake for possible presentation to one of our railway museums is this 1952 income tax slip from the employer - Canadian Pacific Railway Company, Windsor Street Station, Montreal - in the name (wrongly identified, as it happens) of "Mr. W. Wadden, Casual" for the grand sum in "remuneration before deductions" of $88.04 for one month's work. $2.64 was deducted for income tax.

I was so glad to get back home.

2

Apprenticeship

NIGHT WORK AT THE DAILY NEWS

Launching of my relatively brief but lively career in Newfoundland news media began one night in September 1952 at the Duckworth St. premises of the St. John's Daily News. My duties were simply defined as night proof reader, an unglamorous but important cog in the production line for a busy morning newspaper. It seemed to suit me all right - I've always been a bit of a night person - and it fitted in with my daytime schedule as a special student at Memorial University. I had signed up for some English courses to earn credits toward a B.A. degree.

Beginning the work was a bit inhibiting, since I was working under the eagle eye of an irascible night editor, Arch Sullivan, who proved to be a stickler for being on time, and for getting the printed copy letter perfect. Moody and often impatient, he was under pressure to ensure that proofs were read correctly and no errors slipped by to incur the ire of Daily News owners Chancey Currie or his father, Hon. John S. Currie, or scorn from the day shift City Editor, F. Burnham Gill. As things worked out eventually, both Arch Sullivan and Burn Gill became good friends of mine, but in those early days, I wasn't so sure I liked them and, as a greenhorn with all the drawbacks of a college education, gaining some credibility was an uphill battle.

The work wasn't hard, but it was tedious. For five nights a week, Sunday to Thursday, the routine was the same. I'd check in at 11 p.m., take up the tear sheets of copy picked up from the linotype operators, and scour the news columns to spot and mark any mistakes the conscientious linotype operator might have missed. Linotype setting went on until the paper was put to bed, somewhere around 5 o'clock in the morning. By that time, the eyes were getting bleary indeed. Somehow, though, the $35 a week pay packet I earned did seem to make it all worthwhile.

On the night shift, one of my main contacts, apart from the night editor, was Sam Moore, the genial night supervisor of the press room. He ruled the room with a steady hand and a keen eye for ensuring that operations were running smoothly. He was always kind and considerate to me, and welcomed me to his home a few times. He had a warm sense of humour and was a great story teller.

In a gratifying postscript - I got an e-mail from Sam's son, Joe, following publication in the Telegram in 2004 of a "Slice of Life" article mentioning his father which I wrote about my Daily News experience. He said, in part:

> I was the 10-year-old son of Sam who would come down to the kitchen when the Daily News "workers" would come to 5 Hayward Avenue well in their cups, and more houses to go. This happened once a year

Nix in 1950s - typing practice   *(Mary Brown photo)*

around Christmas time. One (story) Dad loved to tell was about a man ... he was in the rats to a small degree and came into the News and told Dad he was 'bothers' because everywhere he went, the Blessed Virgin would be following him, and she was even here now. Dad said to go into the toilet, as no BVM would follow him in there. Well, when he came out he was really delighted and thanked Dad, as the BVM had stopped following him.

Copy for newspaper printing at that time was set by linotype operators working at what I always thought were huge and noisy linotype machines. These guys were intriguing to watch in action, especially one or two, such as Kev Wall, who worked at a phenomenally fast pace. Another was Cyril Power, whom I had known for years as one of St. Bon's best hockey players. I got to play hockey with him and other co-workers that year, me as goalie, on the Daily News hockey team.

One interesting denizen of the night press room staff was Johnny O'Toole, who set the headline type. He was reported to be 84 years old, and had worked at the News for 50-odd years, always on the night shift. A kindly, soft-spoken man, he loved to boast that he'd "never worked a day in his life!"

Other characters were a father and son team, Jack and Frank Crane who, along with Bob Snow, worked on the presses, talking incessantly throughout the night. Jack, a ruggedly handsome, muscular type believed to have been popular with the ladies, had an encyclopaedic knowledge of the St. John's populace. He seemed to know everybody in town, rhyming off family names, brothers, sisters, children, uncles, aunts, cousins and where they lived, what they worked at, and sometimes how much money they made. A born politician if he'd wanted to be.

A nightly ritual was a mid-shift lunch about 2 a.m. when everyone sat around to eat, drink tea or coffee, and smoke and talk. I was a smoker in those days too, but found the going pretty heavy in the confined lunch room quarters we shared. A favourite snack food was smoked caplin, the smoking in this case being accomplished by tossing the dried caplin onto a hot plate. Scorched caplin often resulted, and they sometimes came out downright black, but hungry palates have a way of accepting anything at all sometimes.

Talented writer-reporter Art Pratt was a frequent visitor on the graveyard shift, usually to slip in a late breaking story or a titillating mini-column that he contributed for morning readers. Writing with a great sense of humour, he did a daily 'funny', relating little anecdotes or commentaries on daily life in the old town. One I remember was his description of the Newfoundland Constabulary guard of honour running through their paces for the opening of the House of Assembly at the Colonial Building. Ceremonial rifles borne at shoulder height were fitted appropriately for the occasion, he confided, with newly polished Canadian Javelins. (A reference, for the less mature among us, who never heard the phrase, to the company headed by John C. Doyle, the notoriously dodgy financier involved in various dealings with the Smallwood regime.)

After-hours forays in search of liquid refreshment were an occasional aftermath to night shift stresses, especially when both Art and Arch were together, and I was a willing companion. A call upon a bootlegger usually was required and, as often as not, the locale for sharing cheap rum or whisky was in the back of a car. No scrapes with the law or mishaps occurred as I recall, so it was a merry time mainly given over to stories about townsfolk and politics, the lifeblood of newsy people, especially in Newfoundland. To be sure, the demon drink did its share of damage to both of my companions over the years, but in my limited close acquaintance during those dark dreary nights of 1952-53, they were always friendly, warm-hearted and serious-minded people who cared deeply about justice, integrity and honesty in the public affairs of our homeland. Art went on to join Canadian National Railways as a public relations man in Moncton, N.B. Arch and I worked together in later years, covering House of Assembly sessions for CJON.

Although he could be moody and snappish at times - coming in to work an hour before midnight can tend to make one that way - Arch Sullivan was usually quite pleasant to work with, as long as you did your work. Never burdened by any formal training - he got into news after some time with the telephone company - he had a sure sense of news value, and an abiding passion to see justice done. On the job he hewed to the needs of the moment but, in off hours, did frequent battle with whatever authorities there might be to right a wrong affecting anyone of his acquaintance. Many is the time I saw him grabbing up the phone to call some power figure or another to air a grievance. Given his offbeat work schedule, such phone barrages most often came late, very late, at night. His favourite targets were cabinet ministers, all the way up to the Premier. He'd call Joe (Smallwood) at the drop of a hat. They knew each other from years back, and Arch was a great admirer, but he liked to say his piece, and the Premier, to give him his due, would usually hear him out.

My working relationship with Arch at the News was a good one, and he could be more than tolerant if any problems cropped up, though he had his limits. I found what they were one memorable night when I pulled what I thought at the time was a brilliant coup. I wanted to go to a university dance, but was supposed to work, so I talked a fellow student, "Duck" Moores, into covering for me at the paper that night. I told him the job was simple - just reading a few columns of text and marking in corrections. Trouble was, I didn't tell Arch, or anyone else. Next morning I got two angry phone calls, one from my student friend who was, he said, thrown out of the office the moment old Arch spotted him in my chair. No damn way was a stranger going to be allowed to mark up his copy! My second call was from Arch who, never in the best of humour the morning after, gave me hell for shirking the job and trying to pawn off this other fellow to stand in for me. By the tone of his voice, I fully expected to be fired, which I probably should have been. Fortunately, he let me off with a grim warning never to pull a stunt like that again. Needless to say, my dancing days, or nights, were few and far between for the rest of that year.

There was, come to think of it, one other occasion when I got into hot water. One of the linotype operators - I think his name was Andrews - had the use of a small company van, and once in a while did me a favour by driving me home after work. One night I told him I had forgotten something at my parents' summer place in Kelligrews, 20 miles from town, and could he drive me there during our 2 a.m. lunch break. No problem, he says, I'll take you. He figured it would take no more than half an hour each way. We didn't quite make it that fast, and we were late getting back. When word got around that he took off to drive me out in the country, he was docked some pay. We were both given whatfor and a warning, so we never tried that again.

Truth is, reading proofs was a really boring job, so any excuse to escape from routine was always welcome. A fiendish temptation indulged in a few times was to send back to the linotype operator a deliberately misspelt version of words that came close to one of the more common vulgarisms one hears on the street. It was always a chuckle to see the puzzled look on a cautious operator's face as he questioned that dubious proof mark on a story about the Funk Islands. One of my supposed chores was to proofread the stock market quotations. Lord help market watchers who relied on those the News carried during that period. I scanned the stocks in the most perfunctory manner at the best of times, and not at all when I could get away with it. Didn't hear of anyone jumping off buildings, but I did wonder sometimes...

Needless to say, I can't claim to have learned a lot of journalism in that job, as the most I ever wrote was the odd story header. Yet it was interesting to see what made news and to read the way reporters wrote it. One of the regular segments each night was a two column collection of brief news stories by Jack A. White. His regular job was as news editor at CJON, which had just begun broadcasting in 1951 with a heavy reliance on local news. A real pro reporter, Jack used to work at the Daily News in earlier years. Jack's columns for the News were mainly duplicates of his radio news copy but they made up a good part of the paper's hard news content. Some years later, when I joined the CJON news staff, I came across Jack's old files. Marked for a variety of news outlets ranging from the Toronto Globe and Mail to Time magazine, they held faint carbon copies of identical sets of news columns comparable to those I used to read at the Daily News. Guess it was worthwhile in those days to be a special correspondent.

One of my personal mementoes, incidentally, is a clipping of a Daily News photo story Jack wrote about Boy Scout Apple Day in 1944 - I was one of the uniformed Scouts who sold him an apple. Getting my picture in the paper at that early stage doubtless sowed the first seed of my journalistic aspirations. Jack eventually moved on from journalism to don the robes of a magistrate. Honeymooning in Woody Point, Bonne Bay, in 1959, my wife Madeline and I dropped in for a friendly visit with Magistrate White and his family. I never thought to thank him for the apple story.

Post script # 2: That Daily News article of mine in the Telegram evoked a second interesting e-mail response, this time from Jack White's son, Bliss:

> My mother saw your "Slice of Life" nostalgia story in the January 28, 2004 edition of The Telegram and has provided copies to my three sisters and me. We have all enjoyed reading the piece, particularly your memories of my father.

Those were heady days in which Newfoundlanders deliberated on their place in the world. Dad was proud of being a Newfoundlander and so happy to be a part of all that, to be writing about it to his fellow citizens. I remember being thrilled by Dad's stories from that time - about WW II, the vote choosing Confederation with Canada, the IWA strike, and Joey Smallwood in general, to name a few.

We also have fond memories of our years in Bonne Bay. I would have been about one year old when you and your wife visited as newlyweds. Mom and Dad tell great stories about how cold the house got in winter. A freshly killed chicken hung in the hallway froze overnight, as did water in the toilet. Dad knew so many people. As kids going around on week-end errands, we couldn't get very far before he ran into someone he knew and had a chat.

One of his favourite stories about his years as a Magistrate in Bonne Bay was when he got a flat tire on the (then unpaved) highway between Rocky Harbour and Woody Point. My father readily acknowledged his limited skills at mechanical repair and was contemplating his situation when a passing car stopped. A man got out of it, fetched a tire iron from his trunk and began walking towards my father. As he approached, Dad recognized him as someone he had convicted of a criminal offence some years earlier and sentenced to prison. Whatever apprehensions my father might have had about the man's intentions and armament were quickly allayed when the fellow confirmed his identity, said he thought Dad had treated him fairly, and that Magistrate White would not have to change his own tire so long as he was around.

My sojourn at the Daily News ended in July 1953 when I pondered what to do next while remaining committed to completing courses needed for degree credit. An interim outdoor job cropped up to help fill the gap.

VOCM's FIRST NEWSMAN

The "Voice Of Charlie Mercer", my father used to jokingly call it, Charlie being a prominent store keeper near our summer home at Kelligrews. Never did hear an authentic rendering of the call signal, though it liked to consider itself the "Voice of the Common Man". "VO" for "Voice Of" were the first two call letters of all radio stations in Newfoundland before entry into confederation in 1949. The only surviving commercial station from that era, VOCM enjoys the unique distinction of being the only commercial radio outlet in Canada whose official call letters don't begin with a "C" for "Canada".

And I was VOCM's first ever news reporter! I made my radio debut in September 1953, beginning what was to be a bold but short-lived effort to build a news service from the ground up. A brash ambition for one unburdened with extensive journalistic credentials - an uncompleted journalism course and a stint as Daily News overnight proofreader.

Though in operation for nearly 20 years, VOCM had long relied exclusively for news coverage on a somewhat unique source known as the Terra Nova News Bulletin. Owned, operated and sponsored since 1936 by Harvey and Company, one of Newfoundland's oldest commercial firms, its small staff produced three daily news programs

Nix Wadden at VOCM - checking the wire

broadcast on VOCM. These consisted of 15-minute newscasts at lunch and supper hours, and a repeat of the evening bulletin at 9:45. It was unapologetically patterned after the better known Gerald S. Doyle News Bulletin, a mainstay of what had been the government of Newfoundland's official station, VONF ("Voice Of Newfoundland"). CBC took over operation of this station upon confederation.

Approaching VOCM, I got an encouraging reaction from Mengie Shulman, who did much of the operational management at that time though his main job was advertising. An American who settled in St. John's after putting in army service at a wartime base, he worked in the retail sector as "the Model Shop Man" in 1946 before moving on to VOCM. An aggressive entrepreneur at heart, Mengie was always pushing for new ways to generate business. Tough competition from two-year-old upstart rival CJON, with its boastful slogan "First With the News In Newfoundland", was putting the heat on VOCM's complacent attitude toward community involvement. So, probably because I just happened along at the right time, I was hired to see what news coverage I could develop for broadcast in between Harvey's 1:30, 6:45 and 9:45 News Bulletins.

We began by scheduling newscasts at five minutes before the hour, endeavouring to upstage CJON's report which loudly advertised "news on the hour." One news gathering asset VOCM did have to offer was a set of teletype machines feeding in a constant output of national and world news as provided by Canadian Press and the British United Press. Incorporating these reports made the introduction of newscasts throughout the day a lot easier, although the temptation was always there to rely totally upon "rip and read" content. Since these wire services were geared to newspaper use, they were awkwardly worded for radio, but had to do until staff could be found to rewrite them. But that was not going to happen in 1953.

Working closely with Harvey's News editor Ray Simmons, I tapped into his network of local contacts and out of town correspondents, and introduced brief news casts throughout the broadcast period. As time allowed, I ventured out on daily rounds of primary news sources - police, courts, city council and the like. From the McBride's Hill studios, all were within a few minutes walk but, as a solitary reporter, the scope of coverage was pretty well limited. As a new service, it took time to impress on station staff the need for support and cooperation. Frustrations were many, since all the major news of the day was reserved for coverage on the major news bulletins.

Throughout those early days at VOCM, station operations proceeded under general direction of a largely unseen presence, the founder and managing director, Joseph L. "Joe" Butler. He inaugurated the station in 1933 after working as operator and announcer for VONF, opened the previous year by the Dominion Broadcasting Company, a subsidiary of the Avalon Telephone Company. An austere individual who delivered regular Sunday radio religious readings, he left day to day operations to senior staff. His off hours passion was for flying his own plane, an avocation which ended in tragedy a year later as he crashed while searching for a missing child.

I don't think I ever spoke to Mr. Butler, as we reverently referred to him. He didn't seem to come in very often and, when he did, he kept within closed doors in his office. One presence that was frequently in evidence, however, was his dog. A huge, old, ungainly and foully smelling Newfoundland dog, the creature was known to amble down to McBride's Hill from the Butler home uptown. Unaccompanied - and no wonder - he'd lumber up three flights of stairs of the old Pope furniture building to the VOCM studios, and take up his favourite position, slung off near the top of the stairs outside the boss's office, leaving staff members no choice but to step around or over him. If he had a name, I don't remember it, but the memory, and the odour, lingers even yet!

Perhaps because news activity wasn't working out too well, I seem to remember only a small corps of announce staff at that time. Apart from Mengie Shulman, the only ones I can remember are long time staffer Jim Murdock and Jim Regan, who moved to St. John's from Halifax, partly because his mother came from Cape Broyle. More talent was added later on as efforts continued to improve and expand program services in the face of tough competition from CJON.

Despite determined efforts to bring about a workable news service, my one-man campaign never did pick up much steam. There was limited support or cooperation from management and other staff, except for Mengie, so by December, disillusioned with news work, I decided to quit, and try my luck at something else. Not one of my brightest moves, as things turned out, but something else to chalk up to experience.

Though I did not appreciate it at the time, my labours at VOCM that fall did lay the groundwork for my return to radio news nine months later and, a few years after that, a more promising opportunity to build up a VOCM news operation.

ADVENTURE IN AUDITING

Any good at adding up figures? Without a calculator, that is. You could have a future in auditing. But don't bet on it.

One cold January day in 1954, I entered the Church Hill portals of a respected St. John's firm of auditors, John R. Parsons and Sons, to commence a brief but undistinguished career as an apprentice auditor. A good firm indeed, with many fine and talented employees engaged in checking and monitoring and analyzing the accounting practices of those responsible for making businesses pay a fair profit for services rendered and goods supplied for public use.

Seemed like a smart idea at the time, and it had its good points, to be sure but, alas, as a career development move for me, it turned out to be a positively hopeless giant step in the wrong direction. One in a series of false starts bred no doubt by youthful immaturity and lack of self-confidence. Friends working in the audit field, one of them at Parsons, prompted my curiosity and, when my abortive experiment in radio journalism turned sour, I decided to give number crunching a fling.

A certain facility in mathematics persuaded me that this could be the field for me, foreseeing a succession of problem-solving achievements applying the fruits of recent studies in trigonometry, analytical geometry and the like. Plunged in short order back to earth, I found myself huddled in cramped back office quarters, scanning scores of pages of debit and credit records adding up the old fashioned way, in my head, lengthy columns of figures to check for errors and balance inequities. Assigned at first to genial senior staffer Walter Miller, I picked up valuable tips on skills and systems to learn about, what to look for, and whom to ask any questions. Others filled me on such other essentials as the workings of client firms and the personal idiosyncrasies of staff members.

My fellow workers were a delightful lot, and I got to know many of them pretty well. It was fun to compare notes at times with my old school buddy, Bill Brown, and another St. Bon's graduate, Basil "Butch" Hickey. One of my best pals on and off the job was Duncan "Dunc" Barnes, with whom I did a lot of socializing in town and, thanks to his ownership of a car, around Conception Bay. I even dated Cynthia, our vivacious secretary, a marvellous dancer whom everybody loved but saw her find romance with an interloper from Montreal. Taking in a heady round of dances and parties and meeting our share of interesting and attractive girls made up considerably for what were for me increasingly unsatisfying daily chores.

There was some variety of scene, perhaps - a few days at a time in a wholesale business, or a car dealership, or a heating oil outfit, or a big furniture store. But the work itself, always merely adding up figures. After a while, it proved a great way to catch up on one's sleep. One place I always remember was really great for that escape from reality - it was a long narrow room with no one else about, lights rather low, and my partner and I left conveniently alone to pursue our labours. Since he too was susceptible to the drowsy eye syndrome, there were times when we would both sink into silent slumber. Boredom was never so comfortable.

Waking hours did at times offer a little insight into the gyrations of price-setting for unit sale as against the costs of purchase. Markup levels differed somewhat from one type of business to another - getting a peek at car sale margins gave one pause in after years when contemplating new deals on wheels. None of the markups were quite so staggering, however, as those detected at a suburban furniture warehouse noted for its constant advocacy of cost savings.

There were interesting moments as well. At one location on a busy waterfront street, sidewalks outside office windows were frequented by an astounding succession of colourful town characters, mostly individuals noted for their propensity to alcohol. One office regular regaled us with tales of their rambling lifestyle, as many of them popped in from time to time to solicit a helping hand, or just a moment of warmth on a cold morning. Bearing names of Dashiell Hammett-esque vintage - Tommy Toe, Bingo Kane, Satan, Uncle Billy and the like - they provided a constant source of wonder and amusement amid the grinding monotony of balancing account books. St. John's in that era was a city of characters, widely known and celebrated and indeed beloved for their truly genuine if all too human traits.

Diversions such as this aside, the daily drudgery of low level accounting and auditing practice got to be progressively more punishment than I could take, so I had to discover a way out. Packing it in at last, I dashed off to earn a few dollars the same way as I did on other summer jobs, signing up with Willett Engineering on a highway survey crew at the tail end of Gander Lake. The weather was good, the pay wasn't bad, and I didn't have to add up figures any more. But, as it turned out, this job was even more short-lived. A job opportunity as a radio news reporter came to light in a broadcast report I heard, but that's another story...

TUTORING TIME

Tutoring teen-agers - what did I think I was doing? Emboldened, I suppose, by receiving in the mail my Bachelor of Arts degree certificate. A belated reward for having qualified for the St. F.X.-conferred degree upon earning extra credits for two English literature courses at Memorial, and winning approval of my submitted thesis from Father Bannon, my old English professor. My thesis topic "Satire in the Modern Novel," might well have been applied to the wayward pathway of my career at that period. However, I could now move on, even though just where I still wasn't sure.

It was an uncertain period for me, since I had found more frustration than fun that fall in my four months news writing job at VOCM, and had embarked, in a spur of the moment decision, on a foray into the unknown territory of auditing. This little excursion into part time teaching had to be some kind of safety valve.

Teaching anyone had never been an ambition of mine, though I got a little taste of it during my otherwise sorry sojourn at St. F.X. University. There, I succumbed one day to an earnest plea for help with Latin from my good friend, Fintan Aylward. Bent on earning a Latin credit essential for one aiming at a legal career, Fintan had a lot of trouble with it, and sorely needed help. I worked with him on it, drawing upon my two university credits in Latin and years of it in high school. By hard work and good luck, he managed to gain that pass mark, and he has been thanking me for it for years. Retired by now, I suppose, after a distinguished career as a Supreme Court Judge, he probably doesn't remember a thing about those lessons, but he never forgets what he sees as a friendly deed.

Yet, it must have been a symptom of my desperate state of mind that winter of 1954 when I hung out my modest shingle inviting unwary tutoring clients. Not a shingle, perhaps - just a two inch single column classified ad:

> High School Students!
> Need any help with your Math, French, Latin, English?
> College graduate available evenings and weekends as private tutor.
> Lessons at reasonable cost.
> Phone 4207 at meal hours.

the Colonial Broadcasting System. Its power output in those early days was a mere 100 watts, but was increased to 1,000 watts in 1950. An historic institution in itself, Harvey and Company was a multi-faceted mercantile firm founded in the late 18th century, but keenly intent on keeping in step with the times.

The ancient origins of the old firm yielded an amusing reminder from time to time when I got a phone call from home while working after hours in the office. "Harvey's Pier Two" was the mumbled response my wife heard as the call was answered by an overnight attendant. We always had a great laugh over that when the call was switched over to me.

Working under Ray Simmons' direction, I gradually took over from him most of the news reporting duties, leaving him to concentrate on running advertising programs for the company. His boss, Harvey and Company director Herbert Brookes, was keenly interested in merchandising and marketing enterprises, and gave strong support for building up of the news and advertising services.

Ray Simmons was a very good writer and editor himself, and taught me most of the tricks of the news reporting trade, although he had gotten more involved recently in advertising work. Before meeting him at Harvey's, I had known Ray only as a star basketball player with Prince of Wales College, a member of one of the strongest teams in the inter-collegiate league at that

The people who write your

Harvey's News

RAY SIMMONS
Supervisor

Ronald 'Nix' Wadden, B.A.
Editor

JACK HOWLETT
Sports Editor

JEANETTE PEET
Stenographer

CLAIRE MALLOY
Stenographer

Harvey's News 04   (NW scan)

time. His outside interests while I knew him were mainly to do with sports fishing - he was especially keen about angling for rainbow trout in an obscure pond out Torbay way. Indeed for years he wrote a popular outdoors column in one of the papers. He had a flair for marketing and promotion which fitted in well with the new breed of entrepreneur, such as company director H.H. "Dick" Winter, who were striving to lead the staid old mercantile firm of Harvey's into the mid 20th century. Harvey's Industrial Division was very much an up and coming marketing entity at that stage.

Ray's preoccupation with those aspects of the business gave me full scope for running the news operation, but he gave me every support then and in future years. I owed him many thanks for such confidence, especially on a few dicey occasions when it was most needed.

Before I arrived, Harvey's News Bulletins consisted of the top news stories, which Ray wrote, and secondary content which had been compiled by my predecessor, the late Billy O'Neill. He had been the sole compiler of the bulletin in the early '50s when it was read on air by John Murphy, later to become the Mayor of St. John's. Looking over the past bulletin files, I was appalled to discover that many of these secondary items came from outright cribbing of newspaper stories. Some bulletin pages consisted simply of pasted newspaper clippings. Clearly, this practice had to stop, so one of my first priorities was to do re-writes of any newspaper stories we wanted to use. Having to rely on newspaper content to some extent was hardly avoidable. With more staff and contacts, the Daily News and Telegram clearly had much greater access to news sources, so a little borrowing of content was to be expected. But we didn't have to do it word for word.

Beyond that, the real priority was to go directly to news sources to do our own stories, and that's what I set out to do. My early efforts focussed on covering the major beats and events, setting a regular routine which had me spending as much time out of the office as at my desk. That was the most pleasurable aspect of the work, as it put me in daily touch with news sources, getting to know people and developing personal contacts. Most days I would drop in to the Police Station, sit in for a morning session of Magistrate's Court, and check with the registry staff at the Supreme Court. Every Wednesday I would attend City Council meetings, joining half a dozen reporters following discussions and chatting when possible with the City Clerk E.B. "Ned" Foran and City Engineer Ron Martin.

Sometimes I called in at labour union offices to pick up news and comments which union leaders such as Frank Chafe, Cyril Strong, Larry Daley, Larry Dobbin and Bill Gillies were never loath to offer. Business contacts such as Newfoundland Board of Trade Manager Harry Renouf were contacted regularly. I called frequently at federal government offices - fisheries, public works, labour, harbour pilot, bureau of statistics; and, at the provincial level, municipal affairs, mines and resources, fisheries, labour and many others. A regular and most useful point of call was the office of the Newfoundland Federation of Fishermen, the government-launched organization headed by C. Max Lane and P.J. "Pat" Antle. Getting around to these offices could be time consuming, but made followup phone calling all the more friendly and productive. Over time, of course, I relied more and more on phone calls than footwork, but kept up the personal touch whenever possible.

A good regular information source throughout my news reporting days was the Information Officer of the Federal Department of Fisheries. Mark Ronayne, who had been for years a leading reporter for the Evening Telegram, served in that position in the early 1950s. Always open and thorough in dealing with reporters, he set a high standard for others to follow in government media relations. His boss, Harold Bradley, Regional Director of Fisheries for Newfoundland, also demonstrated keen understanding of the importance of communications, and was always ready and willing to comment and explain any issues or events within his area of responsibility.

In 1956, Mark won appointment to his department's national headquarters in Ottawa, where he became Assistant Director of Information Services. Winning the competition to succeed him was Bruce Woodland, who also displayed top quality skills in that demanding position. He began his career with CBC in Grand Falls, and in 1951 became editor of the Grand Falls Advertiser. Two years later he got an intriguing offer made to him in person by Premier Joey Smallwood during a late night gathering in his Circular Road office. The offer - to become Newfoundland's Director of Tourist Development. A snag developed when the job was given instead to Oliver "Al" Vardy, but Bruce was taken on as his Public Relations Officer. As such he too became for me a regular and valuable new contact, and he remained so during his stint at Fisheries from 1956 to 1959. Toward the end of that year, he transferred across the country to become DFO Information Officer in Vancouver. Jim Quigley performed similar good service as his successor from 1960 to 1966.

Biggest on the spot reporting job, needless to say, was coverage of House of Assembly sessions, and these posed a particularly heavy load. Harvey's News major evening news bulletin aired at 6:45 p.m., and House sessions regularly ran from 3:00 to 6:00 p.m. I covered most if not all of these sessions alone, writing my copy in part in the

House press room and finishing it at the VOCM studio just minutes before air time. This meant a mad dash from the Colonial Building to McBride's Hill each afternoon, writing copy mainly from memory and checking only occasionally with scribbled notes. Handing copy to the news reader - usually the meticulous Denys Ferry - was always a last minute affair, so he had little, and sometimes no, time to read it over in advance. Fortunately, he was a smooth reader, seldom stumbling over what could be rather poorly typed text. (Battered old Remingtons didn't have the seamless self-correction luxury of today's computers.) He gave me hell lots of times for late delivery, but did carry out the job in pro fashion. It was a hectic pace to maintain, but very satisfying indeed at the end of the day.

Harvey's News 01 - Occupational hazard

Workload at Harvey's eased appreciably in March, 1956, when the OK was given to hire a most competent colleague, Jack Howlett, who had spent some years as Sports Editor at the Daily News. He was engaged primarily as a sports reporter but also to assist in Bulletin reporting and editing. Working well together, we managed to divide chores equably and develop notably improved news coverage. Throughout my Harvey's News experience I enjoyed excellent secretarial support, initially from Eileen, wife of VOCM announcer Jim Regan, and later Claire Molloy and Jeannette Peet. Another supportive and friendly presence in the Harvey's office was that of office manager William Rompkey. I knew his son Bill pretty well earlier as a Memorial University student - long before he went on to become a federal M.P. and now a Senator.

20th Anniversary

October 19, 1956 marked the 20th anniversary of both Harvey's News Bulletin and VOCM. A full newspaper spread of news features and advertising formed part of the anniversary celebrations.

Bearing the slogan - Proudly bringing Newfoundland News While It Is News - the Harvey's News ad included the following 'mission statement':

OUR AIM

To bring the people of Newfoundland full, accurate and unbiased reports of all worthwhile news originating within the province.

To carry similar reports of all news concerning Newfoundland or of interest to her people that originate elsewhere.

To serve the people, government departments, charitable organizations, church groups and other people in the propagation of useful information.

To assist Newfoundland and Newfoundlanders in every way possible.

And these things always in compliance with the Broadcasting Regulations of the CBC, with the law of the land and the precepts of fair play and common decency.

THE DIRECTORS
Harvey & Company Ltd.

Rounding Up the News

One regular contributor of Harvey's News Bulletin content was P.E. "Neddy" Outerbridge, reporting on charitable and other activities of the St. John's Lions Club of which he was a staunch member. Accompanied by his driver and sidekick, Jackie Walsh, he dropped by regularly to deliver his Lions reports in person. They were always nicely typed and, in the past, had been customarily incorporated intact in the daily bulletin package.

On perhaps the second occasion I read his report, I ventured to rewrite it, setting the content in what I felt was a more newsy format. O dear! My intervention was not appreciated. My boss, Ray Simmons got an angry phone call protesting vociferously that this "college professor" had had the temerity to interfere with his careful prose. The fact that P.E.O., as he routinely signed his reports, was a brother of two Harvey and Company directors, Herbert and Sir Leonard Outerbridge (then the Lieutenant Governor), called for some diplomacy on Ray's part in dampening his ire. He must have done a good job of it, as no dire consequences resulted and I continued to edit the Lions reports thereafter.

One of the fun chores for me was covering Magistrate's Court. There was always a touch of pain and misery in the line up of cases - break-ins, common assaults, robberies, an occasional robbery with violence and the like. Also an everyday occurrence was the parade of individuals charged with common misdemeanours, usually drunk and disorderly or just plain drunk. The presiding magistrate most of the time, Hugh O'Neill, was a joy to behold in dealing with these offenders. Wryly acknowledging defendants as they shuffled shakily before him, he'd impose the minimum sentence - $10 fine or one month in jail. Sometimes he would wearily urge the miscreant to try a little harder to keep off the stuff.

One recurring offender given a little extra attention was known all over town as Tommy Toe. A chronic alcoholic, he was a harmless character notable for turning up in all kinds of obscure hideaways. A favourite lair was among the rafters of the railway dockyard buildings. On occasion, he raised objection to the charges against him. One day, when asked to identify himself, he answered in an unfamiliar "Tow-mas Ped-dell", both words accented on the last syllable. Repeating this several times, he revealed that he was actually of Portuguese extraction and as such was not subject to the laws of this foreign country. Though eventually convicted and led away, he had court officials and spectators rolling in the aisles and cheering him on for this outbreak of originality on an otherwise slow dry day.

Hughie O'Neill had his sense of humour intact one day when he was challenged by a prisoner accused of being "drunk in a public place". Not denying in the least his inebriated state, the man objected on the grounds that when police picked him up, he was lying partly on a public street and partly on private property. How much of him was on the street, the magistrate asked the arresting officer. About half, the constable replied. OK, the magistrate decreed. You're half guilty. Fine, $5. Stories like this were great to brighten up the usual menu of misery and mayhem common to most newscasts.

An unexpected source of human interest stories was the Supreme Court where registrar Bob Kent and his deputy, Clarence Stirling, were always generous in passing along newsy items. Standard fare was the content of the latest court judgments, the gist of which they would offer verbally while handing over relevant documents. Some dealt with weighty matters of business law suits and obscure legal issues. Of the three Supreme Court judges at the time, those of the Chief Justice, Sir Albert Walsh, were scholarly and succinct. The judgments I liked reading the most were those of Judge H.H. Winter, with very clear, commonsense language. I found those of Sir Brian Dunfield always interesting, but rather opinionated and erratic.

Often of much more public interest was the revelation of the last will and testament of prominent public and business figures, detailing estate value and the various bequests to family or charitable causes. By gathering these items on the spot, I often beat the other media to the story.

On one notable occasion, I found myself in Supreme Court, not as a reporter, but as a prospective juror for a fairly high profile criminal case. When called for confirmation of my suitability as a juror, I began explaining to Chief Justice Sir Albert Walsh that I was a news reporter and... Before I could finish my statement, the chief justice adjourned the session, saying he wished to consult with certain judicial reference tomes in his possession. So I had to wait an hour or so, wondering what this was all about. What I had meant to say was simply that I was a one-man news staff at the time, and I just couldn't do the job if I had to sit on a jury all day long. When Sir Albert reconvened the court, he announced that, after his study of court precedents, he could find no justification for barring me from jury duty because of my journalistic profession, so I was still jury-bound. Within minutes, to my profound relief, defence lawyer Jimmy Higgins stepped up smartly to challenge me, and I was promptly dismissed. An anti-climax, perhaps, but as it turns out, the nearest I ever came to seeing the inside of a jury box.

Pleasant and satisfying as the Harvey's news experience was, it proved often frustrating because important news could not be released immediately because of our separation from VOCM. On occasions when breaking news arrived in our office, we would phone it into the radio station, but with no news staff to handle it, the item might not make it onto the air. On one memorable day, the VOCM phone line was too busy to take a phoned-in tip about a double highway accident fatality on the Burin Peninsula. I got so frustrated that I sent the story by telegram from Harvey's to VOCM - half a dozen blocks away.

Incidents like this prompted serious thoughts about moving the news bulletin service to the radio station. I persuaded Harvey's to support this move and after some negotiations with VOCM management, we got the necessary agreement for the bulletin staff - just me in charge and Jack Howlett as assistant - to become VOCM employees as founders of a VOCM news service, with Harvey's News Bulletin continuing as our flagship responsibility. The changeover Jan. 1, 1957 ended one rewarding news broadcasting experience, but opened the door to another.

Ray Simmons (courtesy Bill Callahan)

Hockey Nights in '55

For nearly four months in 1955, I found myself in the unexpected position of sports reporter for the Evening Telegram. Unexpected for two reasons - first, because I had just been six months on the job as news editor at Harvey's News Bulletin, a job which kept me quite busy indeed, and second, because I had no experience whatever as a sports reporter. However. somebody suggested I might give it a try - I don't really remember who did so - and Steve Herder, the Telegram managing editor - agreed to take me on.

As Steve explained, Harvey Clark, who had been Sports Editor with the Telegram for some years, had quit the job, and they had nobody on the staff to fill in while they were recruiting a replacement. Moreover, this was about the busiest time of the year for sports news, with the hockey season in full swing, and Newfoundlanders were as wild about hockey as any sports fans anywhere. Moreover, the city had just opened the St. John's Memorial Stadium, allowing hockey games to be moved onto a regulation-sized ice surface for the first time. Well, I liked hockey too, and used to play it, as a goalie, in school and university days. Indeed, I still played a bit, being goalie for the

Ishkov Visit Media mingling with Russian Minister: (l-r) a Soviet staffer; Gerry Freeman, Canadian Press; Alan Caule, Telegram; A.A. Ishkov; Sylvia Wigh, Telegram; Nix Wadden, Harvey's News; Don Morris, Telegram; Arch Sullivan, Sunday Herald (NW scan)

Harvey's team in the local commercial league. So, what else could I say?

It helped of course that I didn't have to work nights in my Harvey's job, so it wouldn't be too much of a problem to get to hockey games as needed. Living at the eastern end of Gower Street, I wasn't too far from the Memorial Stadium site beside Quidi Vidi Lake, so I could walk there or get a bus. Just as well because as things turned out, I had to spend a lot of time at the Stadium that winter.

I started on the Telegram sports beat in the first week in February, and had to bone up fast on all that there was to know about league and game schedules, team standings, how to get scoring details and statistics, etc. Much of my time was spent in the Stadium press box where, fortunately for me, I got a lot of help from other reporters and from other regulars who, sometimes for no obvious reason, enjoyed press box access. One of them was George Gillies, father of Ted who was one of the stars of St. Bon's hockey teams which had dominated the city hockey league for decades. Another, Frank "Toe" Byrne, was a fountain of knowledge about hockey and indeed all sports activities.

The St. Bon's - Buchans game

Getting to know something about the current state of city and inter-city hockey was crucial in that early period of my sports writing internship, since it was to be put to the supreme test in only my second week in that role. The date was Feb. 14, and the occasion, an exhibition game between St. Bon's, the top team in the St. John's city league, and the visiting Buchans Miners. The result - a dramatic 3 to 2 upset victory for St. Bon's.

Background to this story is the long and bitter rivalry between those two teams since the late 1940s. The most prestigious athletic award in Newfoundland and Labrador since its inception in 1935 is the Herder Memorial Trophy, emblematic of the all Newfoundland amateur hockey championship. It was created by the Herder family, long time owners of the Evening Telegram, in honour of five family members who served in the First World War. Hockey teams from St. Bon's College, the top Christian Brothers school in St. John's, won the Herder trophy for five years straight between 1936 and 1940, and for another five years between 1945 and 1949. Bell Island was the only other winner in that period, taking it in 1941 and 1944. There was no championship series in two of the war years, 1942 and 1943.

St. Bon's dominance of the provincial hockey scene came to an end after the Buchans Miners team started to import semi-professional hockey players from mainland Canada. Until that time, all hockey players in Newfoundland were strictly amateurs, but there were semi-professional hockey leagues throughout the mainland. Buchans brought in its first imports in 1948. One of the imports was playing coach Frank Bowman. Under his leadership, the Buchans team swept by all opponents to win their first Herder trophy in 1949-50, and were repeat winners in the following two years, and again in 1953-54. Grand Falls also began importing players and captured the championship six times out of seven seasons between 1952-53 and 1958-59.

Although still a leading hockey power in the St. John's hockey league, St. Bon's had failed to compete successfully in inter-town play since the semi-pro invasion. However, the Blue and Gold squad yearned to prove that they were an amateur team which could be a good match for these Buchans upstarts. The Feb 14 exhibition game against the Miners provided St. Bon's with just such an opportunity, though no one really expected them to score a win.

Covering that hockey game was quite a big deal for me, since I was so new to sports writing, I was doing it on my own, and I knew the significance of the game to all sports fans. After the game, I had to do interviews with coaches at a post-game reception held at the Cochrane Hotel, so it was already in the wee hours when I climbed up to the Telegram newsroom to do my story. I was all alone in the Newsroom except for Jim Browne, who covered other sports events for the Telegram and also for VOCM. What with all the excitement of the evening, and no little anxiety about doing justice to the event, writing up the game took me hours to complete. Indeed I barely made it on time for the final deadline which was then about 5 a.m. But it got a good spread, taking up, along with pictures, almost a full page of the paper, and left me tired but satisfied with my night's work. Didn't get a byline, though. Here's how it looked.

Surprise! St. Bon's Pull <u>THE</u> Upset!!
Stadium Couldn't Hold 'em
by Telegram Staff Writer

Victory well-earned!

Can anyone ask for anything more sweet? School ties, rivalries, club or non-descripts, imports, outports, exports...all were forgotten last night when an inspired St. Bon's team did the impossible: they beat Buchans Miners 3-2.

None but die-hard St. Bon's supporters dreamed that the local squad had a chance to win; most hopeful bets were that the city boys wouldn't lose by more than three goals, but still they did it. Well over 5,000 hoarse-throated city fans, plus thousands more by their radios, thrilled with excitement amounting almost to hysteria as the tense, action-packed ice drama unfolded. Paid attendance was 4,982 ... but potential attendance had there been sufficient seating capacity would undoubtedly have gone to double that number; certainly, some 1,500 were turned away when they saw little chance of seeing the game behind the packaged rows of standing spectators.

Most heartening to St. Bon's team was the terrific support expressed in no uncertain manner by the fans. Ardent foes of the Bluegolds during regular city league series joined enthusiastically in lustily cheering on the city lads as they put on a demonstration of sheer fight that hasn't been seen in this capital in many years. Sick and tired of seeing St. Bon's romp to victory in the city league year after year, many fans entered the Stadium determined to cheer for the visitors, but not long after the starting whistle the huge building roared with applause and cheering for the Blue and Gold who, by their spectacular performance, deserved no less. The spontaneous ovation rendered by the standing multitude after the close of the game was as great a tribute, not only to the victors, but even more so to the two fine teams which produced such a satisfying contest, as could ever be spoken by the most eloquent orator.

THE LOSERS

Not since the days of the Old Arena has St. John's seen such a fine team beaten by a city squad. The Miners from Buchans are a strong, fast, smooth aggregation; their pattern of play is unfamiliar to these parts. It is based on speed, most of all, fast breaks, quick long passes to the wing man on the blue line, banging the puck off the backboards, and cutting in for the rebound - but most notably the 'shift.' This brand of play actually resembles the basketball played in the Maritimes; it has the same fast-breaking covered up transfer of the object (in this case, the puck, not the ball) and repeated punching on the goal.

Working the 'shift' most often last night was Hughie 'Red' Wadden, long-legged centreman whose adept stick handling and wound-up rushes across centre ice gave city fans heart spasms every time he tried it. Luckily for St. Bon's, many of these fearsome rushes were blown down for offsides play on the part of his wingmen, who couldn't seem to gauge the play precisely enough to make it effective.

A surprise to fans, who expected fancy stick handling and dazzling shooting on goal, was the tactic tried by Buchans at the start of the game of shooting from just past centre ice into the corners or off the backboards to either side of the goal. Purpose was, it seems, to set up a speedy winger to cop the rebound and flip it out in front of the goal. Here too best laid plans ganged aft aglay, as pass-outs failed to get past the Bluegolds' defence and backcheckers, so after a while this strategy had to be laid aside.

Defensively, Buchans had their opponents baffled early in the game as they strung out forwards and rearguards in what seemed a haphazard line but what proved to be a very effective stopgap to advancing St. Bon's forwards. No sooner was, say, Noel Sparrow up to the Buchans blue line with the puck than he found himself enmeshed by bodies and sticks of three defenders, and rarely could get his pass away.

On the attack, Miners could keep St. Bon's bottled up for more than a minute at a time as they blocked every pass out, zipped the disc back, ahead or sideways to a teammate, and let go with another shot. Only the amazing goal protecting formation of the Bluegolds, and especially the stupendous defensive play of Hugh Fardy, saved Green from a formidable pounding.

Individually it wasn't easy to distinguish the 'local' from the 'imported' players on the Buchans team. Greg Floyd, the goalie, was a pleasure to watch, as he displayed quick reflexes and cool competence on all plays. St. John's boy Bill Scott was as smooth and clever as playing coach Frank Bowman, while all forwards showed up fast and well trained. Only fault the fans could pick up was in the shooting, which was way off on many clear scoring opportunities.

THE WINNERS

In style and pattern of play, St. Bon's largely followed their usual familiar routine, but the way they fought was new, at least for this season. Their foes seemed unprepared for a quick jump to the offensive at the start, and by the time they recovered, St. Bon's were conditioned to the type of play. When hemmed in their own zone, they covered up the goal as they had never done before; still they were always ready and able to leap into a breakaway.

Time and again the sparkling work of Hugh Fardy disrupted Buchans breaks, while the goal-tending of Merv Green was superb. Sure goals in the eyes of despairing fans turned miraculously into routine saves by this rock steady rookie who turned aside more than half a dozen clear breakaways. And Noel Hutton bounced one and all, easily the game's best checker. Other than these, no other Bluegold man needs individual mention, for every single one turned in the hardest working and best game of his career. All played 100 per cent of their capacity and no more than that could anyone ask.

Team line-ups:

St. Bon's: Merv Green, Hugh Fardy, Noel Hutton, Cyril Greene, Len Coughlan, Bill Organ, Ted Gillies, Jack Reardigan, Noel Sparrow, Jim McNamara, Noel Vinnicombe, Cyril Power, Bill Corbett, Mort Ryan, Ed Manning, Jack Vinnicombe (Coach).

Buchans: Greg Floyd, Ron Mullins, Bill Scott, Frank Bowman, Al Mullins, Herb Pike, Will Harris, Hugh Wadden, Jim Hornell, Danny McNeil, Doug McNeil, Tony Walsh, Dan Bisson, Pat Kennedy, Jack Cooper, Tubby St. George, Roy Mullins, Gus Soper (Manager)

Hugh Wadden

For me personally, the most interesting Buchans Miner hockey player was Hughie Wadden, mainly because we had the same surname. For that reason, I sought him out during one of the social gatherings held during their St. John's visit. He came from a coastal community called Port Morien in Cape Breton. I knew there were Waddens in Cape Breton but had never met one of them before. Wadden is not too common a name anywhere - most of those in Newfoundland are related to me in some way - and we have one other thing in common - we're all Catholics. The Cape Breton Waddens, however, are Protestant, and I'd often wondered if there was any link between the two family groups. Well, talking to Hughie did not shed much light on that question, but we had a nice chat and enjoyed exchanging a little information about our families.

According to my brother, Brian, our family historian, there was indeed a link between the two Wadden groups, and his name was Ben.

He was recruited in St. John's in 1795 by the Royal Nova Scotia Regiment, which had been sent to help protect Newfoundland during the Napoleonic wars. He returned with the regiment to Cape Breton where, a few years later, he received a land grant in what is now the Port Morien area. (Hughie must be one of his descendants!) One of his sons, also named Ben, settled in a nearby cove which became known as Wadden's Cove. Somewhere along the way, the family members turned Anglican to comply with the prevailing religion of that area. (Years later, my family and I visited Wadden's Cove and met one of its few remaining residents, Minnie Wadden Boutelier.)

Nightly Routine

After such an exciting highlight event, hockey reporting got to be a relatively routine activity for the rest of that winter season. What with the city league, periodic inter-town games, inter-collegiate competitions, as well as commercial league events, there was a steady round of game reports to compile. I went to the more important games, but after a while looked for ways to maintain coverage without spending seven nights a week dashing between the stadium and assorted rinks around town.

Then I found an ally. There was this guy who seemed to be always at the games, and was always keenly interested in picking up score sheets afterwards. Try as I might, I do not recall his name. Seeing each other often, we got to chatting a lot and at one point he made me an offer I couldn't refuse. He offered to pick up the game sheets and deliver them to me after the games, saving me the time and trouble of going to the site.

Now it so happened that I was not infrequently inclined to drop into the Cochrane Hotel at night for a beer and a chat with friends, most of them being former classmates and pals of mine from Memorial University. The Cochrane was our favourite watering hole, and it stood just two minutes from my family home on Gower Street. So the rest was easy - I would relax with my companions for a couple of hours, and, between 10 and 11 p.m., my helpful hockey records collector would turn up, hand me over the score sheets, tell me some of the game highlights, and I'd be all set to go to the Telegram and pound out the night's sporting news. I'd feel a mite guilty about it sometimes - the most I could do for my benefactor was buy him a beer once in a while. He just loved doing this, and I guess got a kick out of helping to make the news.

My dalliance with sports reporting ended when the Telegram, at the end of May, found someone to take on the sports beat. That someone was 14-year-old Max Keeping who, then still at school, had begun covering high school sports for the Telegram. He made such an impact with his reporting skills that within two years he was appointed sports editor. By 1961, he was with VOCM, doing news, sports, and music, and in 1963 he headed for CJCH in Halifax to work on news, sports and open line shows. He moved to Ottawa in 1965 to become CFRA Radio's first Parliamentary correspondent. A year later he joined the CTV news staff as a hill reporter. He moved on in 1972 to become news director and anchor for CJOH-TV in Ottawa. Along the way he became one of the national capital's best known and most successful fund raisers and public personalities, averaging over 200 public appearances a year. He was appointed as a Member of the Order of Canada in 1991 and, among his many honours is a Gold Ribbon Award from the Canadian Association of Broadcasters for outstanding community service, and induction into the CAB's Hall of Fame.

MY FIRST CAR

I bought my first car June 13, 1955, when I was working at Harvey's News, and just after completing my part-time sports reporting gig with the Telegram. It was a two-door 1952 Chevrolet which I bought from Terra Nova Motors for $1,364.75 (3% sales tax included.)

I sometimes look back on that purchase with lingering regret. Not because the car wasn't OK, but when I think of something else I might have done with the money. My down payment - $300 - had been intended for quite another purpose. I was saving it up to go to Grenoble.

Going to a university in France was a dream of mine ever since my ignominious departure from St. F.X. University. Having made up for lost ground with extra credits enough to earn that elusive B.A., the yen to make another stab at academic success still persisted. Though English was my major, French had been a particular interest at university, and I had three course credits behind me - pretty well all for literature rather than for marketable skills in dialogue and conversation. So, what to do? One of my university teachers had encouraged me to pursue my interest in French, and sang the merits of the University of Grenoble which he had attended in the south of France. I got some information on it, and thought I might have a chance to gain admission There was just the question of money to go there and cover whatever the costs were.

Further encouragement came to me from a former neighbour, Sidney Woods, who had enrolled the previous year at the famous Sorbonne University in Paris. Responding to my letter seeking some advice, she wrote back with lots of basic information, plus tips on how to pare costs and maybe earn a few sous on the side. She told me that getting into the Sorbonne would be no problem: "If one has a B.A., one just turns up and registers, and that's that." She recommended a one-year certificate course that she was taking herself, and gave me details on living costs ($80 a month for her), but stressed that almost everything in Paris was quite expensive. Grenoble might be better than Paris "if you want to be sunk into a French atmosphere, but frankly, if you only have a year or so at your disposal, you would be foolish to miss Paris! It has everything for all tastes, whether you are a goldfish fancier or a drug-addict, a jazz devotee or a balletomane." Being none of the above, I would opt for Grenoble, a mountain area in sunny Province.

I was getting enthusiastic, and putting away a few dollars to go toward it. Earning extra money at the Telegram that winter made a difference. Seeing the bank balance rising to something like $400 - a big sum considering my regular pay was about $50 a week - was bringing the dream a lot closer to reality. Living at home helped a lot - I could walk to work; Harvey's was only 10 minutes from 34 Gower St. (and the Telegram only 15 minutes); and apart from having a few beers and smoking less than a pack a day, I didn't have much to spend money on. Maybe I could make it.

But alas, though the spirit was willing, the flesh was all too weak. Watching all the cars buzz by as one strolled the streets got to be a lure I couldn't withstand, so I made that fateful move. My Grenoble nest egg disappeared into the down payment, and the rest was history. Decades later, grumping about the career limiting strictures of official bilingualism, I rued the day I bought that Chevrolet. Did get to France a few times, and spoke a little French, but still haven't made it all the way to Grenoble. But I'll make it yet!

LONDON THEATRE AND THE LIONS

One of my treasured souvenirs of 1956 is a Daily News clipping headed "The Lion's Share", presenting a tongue in cheek commentary - composed by me under a pseudonym - on a cultural event of high significance in that era. St. John's cultural life throughout the 1950s was vastly enriched by continuing performances by the London Theatre Company, a troupe of professional actors from Britain headed by actor-manager Leslie Yeo. The talented group took up residence in the city in 1951, producing and performing a solid program of live theatre presented in the Bishop Feild College auditorium. After five years of reasonable success, its fortunes had begun to dim, as audiences declined in number, partly due to the advent of television. The company appealed strongly for help from whatever quarter might be available.

Although often a willing and satisfied audience member, I detected more than a little self-serving hypocrisy in the public utterings of some unlikely business and community groups rushing to offer solutions to London Theatre's plight. The last straw for me was this dramatic news item, regarding its Feb. 27-March 3, 1956 production of "When We Are Married":

"Members of the Lions Club and their wives will attend Monday night's performance by the London Theatre en masse. Earlier this week Mr. Leslie Yeo advised that this may be the Theatre's last season in St. John's unless another 500 patrons attend regularly." This momentous event, I decided, called for nothing less than a suitably solemn epic:

THE CHARGE OF THE LIONS BRIGADE

'Alf a buck, 'Alf a buck,
'Alf a buck onward,
Into the Valley of Debt
Strode the Five Hundred.
Forward the Lions Brigade!
Into the Valley of Debt
Strode the Five Hundred.

"Forward the Lions Brigade!"
Was there a check displayed?
Not tho' the cashier knew,
"Just cash" he thundered;
Theirs not to make reply

44

Theirs not to reason why
Into the Valley of Debt
Trudged the Five Hundred.

Culture to right of them,
Culture to left of them,
Culture in front of them,
Bellowed, e'en blundered;
Roared at with cockney crow,
Bravely they faced the show
Into the Jaws of Les
Into the mouth of Yeo
Stared the Five Hundred.

Flushed all their spouses fair
Flushed as, with redding ear,
Words not so nice they hear,
Mixed with the culture, while
All the pit wondered.
Later 'tween acts they smoke,
Gossip 'bout footlight folk,
Lioness and Lion;
Ne'er unkind word they spoke,
"Don't want them going broke,"
Then they rushed back...but not
Not the Five Hundred.

Culture too fast for them?
Culture too slow for them?
Culture beyond them?
'So what?", Les thundered;
Saved from the Debtor's cell,
"E'en while the Teevees sell,
We that had done so well
Came through the Jaws of Debt
Back from the Mouth of .... well!
All that is thanks to them,
Thanks to Five Hundred.

"When can their glory fade?
O the fine role they played!"
All the cast wondered.
Think of the haul we made,
Honour the Lions Brigade,
Noble Five Hundred!"

"With apologies to no one - Ned Daw." as the credit line read.

ST. JOHN'S WANTS ITS LIVE ENGLISH THEATRE

By SYLVIA WIGH

THE theatre has had its ups and downs, and it is not very often that a whole city campaigns to save a theatrical venture from becoming a financial nightmare.

But this is just what happened to St. John's in February of this year. The first indication that all was not well came from an editorial written by Leslie Yeo, General Manager of the London Theatre Company, St. John's, a professional repertory company which has been visiting annually for the past five years.

"Is this to be the last theatre season in St. John's? After five successive years is the London Theatre sign above the entrance to Bishop Feild Hall about to be dimmed forever?" So wrote Leslie, and that was enough to start a small scale avalanche. Business firms and private citizens, school girls and university students, advertising concerns, press and radio all immediately turned on the heat. Offers of asistance came from all over, and were of all kinds.

Ordinary theatregoers offered financial assistance, Memorial University offered free advertising in its annual magazine, daily papers carried news releases, editorials and pictures, radio and television made hourly spot announcements, men's service clubs arranged to attend the theatre with their wives and families, women's clubs followed suit, every theatregoer made it his business to bring another member into the fold and to keep

Leslie and Hilary Yeo at home : Newfoundland?

him there. One shop even offered free flowers to dress the stage for the remainder of the season.

That St. John's realized just what live theatre meant to it was a concrete fact, proven by its actions. As Leslie has previously said on many occasions, television was a factor to be reckoned with, and all over the world the theatre was fighting a battle. Playhouses with proud histories of years of play-producing are closing their doors all over England and the United States, and it could

be expected that the pattern would be repeated here in St. John's.

But there is one factor that makes us unique. While we have taken to television, we are not willing to give up our first love—the theatre. We are a people who wish to have our cake and to nibble at it as well.

As every amateur knows, producing a play is costly business. How much more then must professional theatricals cost? Leslie estimates that it takes $2,500 weekly to keep his company going. The initial expense

in bringing the company out from England is one of their heaviest, and of course the high cost of living in the city is another. That no member of the London Theatre Company is ever likely to retire a wealthy person is one sure thing. They get precious little out of the venture but hard work (and more hard work) and a sense of fulfillment when they see their audience week after week returning to enjoy their performance. That the stage as a profession requires dedication has been said, and

it can be truly said of our own professional company that they are dedicated to their art. They would have to be. They get little else sometimes!

* * *

St. John's has had a proud theatrical history. The first group of visiting players sought permission from Governor Gower in 1806 to present their "Theatrical Representations" in the city. As long as there was a regimental garrison stationed in the city, there were dramatic productions staged by them. Mention was made of presentations in the Globe Theatre, in the Amateur Theatre and the New Amateur Theatre. Visiting players from the United States paid a visit in 1842.

Getting nearer to our own times, the well remembered Glossop-Harris Company brought Shakespeare and contemporary plays during the twenties, followed by a gap of twenty years when the Alexandra Players paid us a visit, numbering among

the manager's editorial brought results

(Continued on next page)

11

London Theatre   (NW scan)

46

Whatever feedback may have resulted from this ditty never got back to me. One person only - I think it was my onetime Daily News colleague Art Pratt - rightly traced the origin of the piece to me, remarking that there lots of Dawes but no "Daw" family name in the area, and "Ned Daw" was "Wadden" spelt backwards.

Despite or because of efforts such as that recounted here, community support did enable London Theatre to remain in business in 1956, but it gave up the ghost a year later. Most of its members moved back to Britain or on to greener cultural pastures elsewhere - Leslie Yeo and his wife and co-star Hilary Vernon settled in Toronto - but some stayed in Newfoundland permanently. One, John Holmes, went to CBC after a brief stopover at VOCM where he picked up a smattering of news editing knowhow during my watch. He took an active part in amateur theatre for many years. Another finding a new career at CBC was Charles Mardell who put in some years as its station manger in Gander.

As a further postscript to this story, I accidentally came upon in Stratford, Ont. a few years ago Leslie Yeo's delightful autobiography "A Thousand and One First Nights", published in 1999. In it he recounts in admirable detail the full story of the London Theatre Company's career in St. John's and brief adventures elsewhere in Canada. Alas, "The Charge of the Lions Brigade" failed to rate even a mention in this excellently written volume.

THE FOUNTAIN

Of all the foibles and follies with which the Smallwood government annoyed and even enraged the populace of St. John's, none came in for more satiric crossfire than what everyone called simply "The Fountain". Typical was this minor gem presented on VOCM in the 1:30 p.m. edition of Harvey's News Bulletin June 7, 1956:

> The quarter-million-dollar fountain - otherwise known as "that monstrosity" - which has been built in front of the House of Assembly - will be ready to operate this weekend. Designed for - oops, by - the CMIC - one of the government sponsored new industries, the "William Carson of Bannerman Park" will be launched as soon as the government is able to sell its latest bond issue.

Meanwhile CMIC - there's no "O" in that, mind you - is busy removing those unsightly trees from the front of the Assembly grounds - this move being taken, no doubt, to give the proprietor of the Colonial Store a better view of members being drenched at the entrance to the legislature.

Reliable sources, meanwhile, intimate that the two big guns - relics of the war of independence - financial independence, that is - now pointing menacingly at the top of the South Side Hills - are to be trained at the Gate of the Assembly grounds to warn off small fry who might be tempted to sail their boats on the Fountain. In other words, this is NOT to be the Fountain of Youth.

Multi-coloured lights representing all shades of political opinion - with Red left out of course - have been installed at the base of the pile - oops, monstrosity - oops, fountain. The ultimate aim being to make this a rival of Cavendish Square. Of course, there's no room for traffic in the grounds, but who cares?

Other reliable sources indicate that television crews and photographic teams from the various atomic energy research boards of the world are to be gathered for the great unveiling - preliminary tests have given every indication that the first gushing from the fountain will eclipse for ever the mild mushrooming of everything from Old Faithful to the Hydrogen bomb at Bikini. And speaking of bikinis, let us once more stress the fact that bathing is absolutely not permitted in this monument to irresponsible government in Newfoundland.

A Visit from Mr. Fishkov

One of the more interesting visits to Newfoundland by a foreign government official occurred in the summer of 1956 when the Soviet Union's Minister of Fisheries came to town. The Hon. A.A. Ishkov, as he was named, became inevitably "Mr. Fishkov" to us news reporters assigned to cover his words and actions. The visit was a double-barreled one, since he was accompanied by the Canadian Minister of Fisheries, Hon. James A. Sinclair of Vancouver. In fact, Ishkov's visit followed a trip which Sinclair made to the USSR in the previous year. (Sinclair, by the way, gained a measure of fame for quite a different reason in subsequent years, when his daughter, Margaret, suddenly married Prime Minister Pierre Elliot Trudeau.)

The arrival of Soviet fishing vessels on the banks of Newfoundland had its start in that year, and there is no doubt that Ishkov and his colleagues were able to apply much of what they learned to the development of their fleet's activities. Had everyone known at the time how devastatingly far-reaching the Soviet and other foreign fishing operations would have on the Newfoundland fisheries, the welcome given its Minister might have been a tad less generous. Ishkov's position as Soviet Minister of Fisheries was actually more closely equivalent to that of a Deputy Minister in the Canadian government, as he was not part of the inner cabinet circle surrounding the Soviet Premier. We were told that he had served in this post for something like 30 years.

Hospitality was the watchword for that event. Media as well as industry representatives mingled with the Soviet Union officials at a big reception at the Newfoundland Hotel, tendered by the Nfld. Fish Trades Association and the Newfoundland Associated Fish Exporters Association (NAFEL). Some of us media types who gathered around the Soviet Minister for a publicity photo seemed to be lacking somewhat in appreciation of the solemnity of the occasion.

Following meetings and information briefings in the capital, Messrs Ishkov and Sinclair and their colleagues were airlifted to Fortune at the tip of the Burin peninsula to see what a real Newfoundland fish plant looks like. We reporters gamely tagged along in an accompanying aircraft. The air trip was a memorable one, as we went by flying boat, landing in pontoon-equipped aircraft on the choppy waters of Fortune Harbour. The passengers all had to be carefully helped ashore from rocking pontoons on to rollicking dories and finally on to comfortably solid dry land.

During a road trip that was part of the Burin peninsula tour, I was intrigued to notice one of the Russian party whose dark visage and full moustache gave him a striking resemblance to Soviet leader Joseph Stalin, who had died three years earlier. I remarked on this to him but I might as well have kept it to myself, as he pretended not to have heard me. The old dictator's popularity had seemingly faded under the regime of his successor, Nikita Kruschev.

4

Sidelines

HERE IN NEWFOUNDLAND

In many ways, at least from the comfortable vantage point of retrospect, 1956 was one of the better years during my media career in St. John's. My work at Harvey's News was very satisfying as I covered all the major news of the day and took part in news conferences, media outings and social gatherings of media people. I got time as well to gain freelance experience, particularly with emerging new local publications. And best of all, I met and began courting Madeline Roche, my future wife, then working as secretary to Evening Telegram publisher, Jim Herder.

In February an Evening Telegram report announced the birth of a brand new magazine, *Here in Newfoundland* published by two 20-year-old entrepreneurs, Edsel Bonnell and Gerry Peet. "Local Boys To Publish Magazine", a newspaper headline put it. It was described as a "behind the scenes" magazine, featuring the writings of Newfoundland's best known journalists and writers. Ed Bonnell was then a Telegram news editor while his partner was an advertising space salesman and layout man with E.C. Boone Advertising Limited.

Here in Newfoundland magazine attracted articles from most of the leading journalists and writers of that time - among them Jack A. White, Don Morris, Sylvia Wigh, A.B. "Arch" Sullivan, Tony Thomas, Aubrey Mack, John Puddester, George Perlin, Michael Stewart, Marguerite Reid, Paul O'Neil, Harry R. Burton, Bill Callahan, Cy Fox, D.W.S. Ryan, Darce Fardy, and others writing under various pseudonyms. I wrote several feature articles as well as a few columns published under the heading Sort Points. This soubriquet I occasionally used in later years for letters to the editor on political issues. This was a fairly common practice during that period, helping journalists and others to blow off steam without jeopardizing their day jobs.

Seven editions of *Here in Newfoundland* were published in 1956, but the ambitious publishers could never raise enough advertising revenue to sustain its growth, so the magazine folded with the December issue.

Here in Nfld   *(NW scan)*

THE SAGA OF SAGEBRUSH SAM

(For the first issue of *Here in Newfoundland* in April, 1956, I contributed a feature story on VOCM's newest and most colourful radio personality widely and fondly known as "Sagebrush Sam." Following is an abridged version of that article.)

Valentines from secret admirers to their favourite radio announcers were far from uncommon at the VOCM studios, but this one was a bit of a mystery" "To Paint Brush". Heads nodded dubiously, and the anonymous card was just about to be cast aside when along came a chubby young man with curly russet-hued hair and said: "Golly, this must be for me!" Sure enough, it was. For Sagebrush Sam was getting used to mix-ups in his name. It was confusing indeed but what, after all, did that matter when a fellow was liked by his listeners? On that point, there was little doubt.

Starting with a 50 minute Western Show, a few records, a guitar and no sponsor, he had caught the imagination of thousands with his style of singing and his contagious laugh. Word of this new radio performer was quick to spread, and mail was pouring in. He was also heard on a breakfast show, and then, on a ten-minute quiz show on which he was known as "Sam, the Rainbow Riddle Man". Burdened with no need for box tops or labels, the show was an immediate hit. In its first week, over 700 answers were received, and the number doubled the

"Sagebrush Sam": Memory of a Muddy River?

Sagebrush Sam

(NW scan

53

next week. Here indeed was a radio personality to be reckoned with.

Inevitably the questions were asked: Who is this Sagebrush Sam? The answer briefly - Omar Blondahl, 33, single, born Saskatchewan, travelled Canada, U.S.A. (Hollywood), Mexico, radio singer, song writer, short story writer, nice guy.

Six months ago he decided to come to Newfoundland. The wealth of folk songs in this oldest colony and newest province he had heard of many times (though he heard his first Newfoundland song after landing on our shores!). He looked up a radio log for the names of stations operating here and - intrigued by the "V" sign (all others in Canada having call letters beginning with "C") he wrote to VOCM. The reply from station manager Harold Butler was favourable, and he arrived in St. John's Christmas Eve. The next day he couldn't find a restaurant open, and had to make his Christmas dinner on apple pie and a coke!

A scant three months later, the newcomer was making arrangements with a mainland recording company for production of a long-playing record containing eight or ten of his renditions of Newfoundland folk songs. That record incidentally is due to come out this month. The wandering troubadour had come a long way.

To get to the beginning of the "Sagebrush Saga", we have to travel back over the centuries, across a patch of ocean to another island - the Vikings-settled isle of Iceland. There for a thousand years had bred a people of fair hair and bright dispositions. In the Scandinavian way, these people followed a practice which was the bane of family historians - surnames did not remain constant, but were forever changing: John, the son of Eric, was known as John Ericson, but Olaf, the son of John, became Olaf Johnson. In Iceland, only a very few families kept the same surname through the centuries. And one of these possessed a stronger tie with history - they, the Blondahls were the pastors of the flock, the Lutheran Ministers. So it was all down the line for centuries, but not all the way.

Came the twentieth century, and the current Blondahl was at odds with the family tradition. He looked, not backward into history, but westward to Canada, the Land of Opportunity. And to Canada he went, taking with him his wife and four children, three boys and a girl. They headed west and settled at last with others of their nationality in the small prairie town of Wynyard, Saskatchewan. And there, in 1923, was born their only Canadian child, a boy. The parents, no doubt with a thought for their far off homeland, called the boy Omar, a name which in Icelandic means "Memory". (Blondahl, by the way, means "Blended, or Muddy, River" - so perhaps a loose interpretation of the boy's name would be "Memory of a Muddy River!")

Until his sixth year, Omar spoke nothing but Icelandic, as did all his neighbours. ..even as he was learning to speak and write English, he was practising an even greater language - music. Omar learned piano, violin, and other instruments, and also had several years vocal training. By the time he was sixteen, the family was living in Winnipeg. His education completed, he looked about for a job, and found one to his liking - acting with the CBC. Dramatic ambitions, however, gave way before the lure of adventure and in 1941 Omar enlisted in the Army. He returned to Winnipeg to find his mother in failing health, and father gone back to Iceland, where he served throughout the war as Icelandic interpreter for the British Government. Omar got another job, but when his mother died later that year, he quit and moved on to Saskatoon to take his first job with a radio station.

The next seven years saw him moving from station to station, all the time developing his music, and turning his hand to the guitar, and his vocal cords to folk music. He worked in New Westminster, B.C. for a few years, and later joined a newly-opened station at Dawson Creek, B.C. His was the first voice to be heard on that station, which was started by a woman. Finally, he landed an announcing job with the biggest station in Edmonton, Alberta - Station CFRN. A high point in his career was soon to come.

1950 was the year when the Canadian Poliomyelitis Foundation was organized, and the year of the first Canadian March of Dimes. All radio stations got together with a big contest to see who would collect the most donations. The contest was to run for three weeks, and at CFRN, the whole campaign was run by Omar in three Saturday broadcasts. He called upon everybody to get behind the drive, and suggested that business firms and organizations vie with one another to see who would devise the most unique way of sending in their contributions. The idea caught on, and from the start the Edmonton station was running neck and neck with a big Toronto station, CKEY. But the money was pouring into Omar in the most unusual forms.

By contest deadline, CKEY Toronto had collected $9,000, far more than any of its rivals in the big city. But when final returns were in, it was left far behind as CFRN stole the prize with a total collection of over $16,000! The victory caused such a stir that Horace Brown, founder of the March of Dimes, flew out to Edmonton to receive the cheque from Omar.

A surprising anti-climax came when he found himself being sent to Hollywood. His one-man feat in copping the March of Dimes contest led a reporter on the Edmonton Sun to write a series of articles about him. In one article, the suggestion was made that Omar should go to the film capital and the idea caught on. Coupons printed in the paper under the heading "Let's Send Omar to Hollywood" were filled out by enthusiastic citizens and shoe boxes full of them flocked in. Before he knew what was going on, the 27-year-old "Scandahoovian" was rattling along the road to Hollywood. The movie capital continued to lure the young Canadian troubadour for the next two years, but at last the glitter was off, and he went to Kelso, Wash.

There he met an old friend, Guy Christian, who bore a striking resemblance to Burl Ives. The two of them teamed up with a travelling group of entertainers, "Smilin' Ernie Lindell and His New England Barn Dance Jamboree Gang", and took to the road. Playing the fiddle and putting on his own ballad singing act, Omar stayed with the gang until late 1955, when he decided to come to Newfoundland.

Omar has often been told locally that he sounds much like Burl Ives, the famous American folk-singer, and he always responds by saying "That's the best praise I could want from anyone." He means it too. Burl Ives is his ideal, 'a man who sings folk songs like no one else in the world." Ives to him is "not only the best, but the only professional folk singer." Perhaps it's a token of his reverence for the American, but Omar usually sports a beard and moustache and, with his chubby face, there is no small resemblance. In his show business career, he has shied away from the cowboy hat and other trimmings of the hillbilly singer, but settles for the beard, a colourful plaid shirt, and a scarf tied about his neck.

In the course of his wanderings he has built up quite a repertoire of folk songs. He knows 200 of them by heart, and carries with him copies of hundreds more. He likes to revive the old songs such as Big Rock Candy Mountain, Foggy Dew, Little Mohee, and has a goodly supply of such offbeat tunes as Giddy-ap Napoleon, I Know an Old Lady Who Swallowed a Fly, Dingtoes, My Cross-Eyed Girl, etc. He's also written some of his own.

Not the sort to plan diligently ahead, Omar yet has some thoughts about the future. One of his reasons for coming to Newfoundland was to be within reasonable distance of the home of his forebears - Iceland.

He himself made a short visit there when he was 14, and most of his relatives are there today. He'd like to go back, but only for a visit.

POSTSCRIPT

An unexpected sequel to the publication of the Sagebrush Sam article popped up out of the blue more than 30 years later when I received a phone call one evening from Vancouver. The date was Aug. 30, 1987, and the caller was Omar Blondahl, from whom I had not heard a thing since years before I moved away from St. John's in the mid 60s. I was not at home when he called but my son, Ron, who was 22 at the time, answered the call. He actually recognized Omar's name from the LPs recorded for Rodeo Records during Omar's years in Newfoundland. We played those records often in our home.

When I called him back, Omar asked if I would be able to send him a copy of the Sagebrush Sam article for use in supporting a proposal he was making for a Canada Council grant related to his musical endeavours. Fortunately for him, my packrat tendencies ensured that I had kept a copy of the magazine and, after much burrowing into musty file boxes, I found it OK. Sent a photocopy off to him and received a warm thank you letter a few weeks later. Heard from him again briefly that Christmas but never did learn whether his Canada Council pitch had succeeded. I understand he died in 1993. "The Man Who Sang Goodbye", a moving radio documentary on Omar's life by Chris Brookes underlined his significant contribution to the popularization of Newfoundland folk songs and pondered the mystery of his total withdrawal from music and his relatively secluded way of life in later years.

Memorial University folklorist Neil Rosenberg, whose interviews with Omar formed the basis of Chris Brookes' documentary, published in the Canadian Journal for Traditional Music (1991) an article entitled "Omar Blondahl's Contribution to the Newfoundland Folksong Canon."

Newfoundland Weekly

Alternative newspapers designed to compete, albeit on a small scale, with major dailies and well established weeklies, have cropped up every few years, but few if any have survived for any length of time. A listing of Newfoundland periodicals compiled by Memorial University shows an astonishing number of such publications, many of them designed to express a political viewpoint.

One of these was the Newfoundland Weekly, which came out with its first issue Dec. 15, 1956. It origins were reported in a Telegram story Nov. 22, headed "CJON Staff Quits to Found Weekly Newfoundland Newspaper."

Founders were Jim McGrath and Art Harnett, who ran a strong but unsuccessful campaign in Harbour Main district in the Oct. 2nd provincial election, and Bren Walsh. McGrath had been in advertising sales at the station, Harnett was a staff announcer and special events producer, and Walsh was news director. With Bren Walsh as editor, the Weekly sought to project itself as non partisan, but actively investigated and reported on a variety of scandals and dubious dealings in provincial government programs and contracts.

I contributed a few news items as the Weekly got established, and by summer 1957 I initiated my own column under the title of "Town Crier", and the pseudonym "Lard". It even got an introduction from the Editor:

> This week the NEWFOUNDLAND WEEKLY celebrates the birth of a new baby in the person of Town Crier. We don't know what he will be writing about every week from now on but we can promise that it will be lively and calculated to keep you on your toes if you enjoy controversy. So welcome to our paper, Town Crier, and all we have to say in the way of potential censorship is that we can permit only the mildest of libel. Otherwise, anything goes.

The first column appearing August 1, 1957, posed the question:

> Is this town big enough to have two weekly papers? This question greeted the advent of the NEWFOUNDLAND WEEKLY last December, and is still being debated over morning coffee at McMurdo's. Many are surprised the WEEKLY has lasted so long. Why has

it? We suggest the answer lies in the present journalistic situation in Newfoundland. The people need another voice!

Did you know the Telegram's editorials are practically all written by the same person who writes its daily column: Harold Horwood? Did you know the Daily News editorials are all written by the same person who writes its daily column: Albert Perlin? Everyone knows the Sunday Herald is owned and operated by CJON, although its editorials and the bulk of its story material are written by Editor Arch Sullivan, whereas Don Jamieson dictates the editorial policy of CJON. Not to mention the fact that the Western Star at Corner Brook, Nfld.'s only other newspaper of any general influence, is owned by the Telegram. VOCM in St. John's indulges in no editorializing, aside from the occasional theatrical "aside" from News Announcer Denys Ferry. CBC, being a drain upon the Canadian taxpayer, risks no comment on the status quo.

WEEKLY has added a new Voice, independent of all other media, and injecting a fresh note between the cautious fence-straddling of the News and the iconoclastic "gang busting" of the Telegram. Editorials, however, are limited in their scope, and essentially authoritative, or should be....

Another Town Crier column offers a contemporary view on politicians at the municipal level:

Something new has been added to pow-wows of the City Council these past few months, and the man to thank for it is the Junior Councillor, Alex Henley. The "something" new and unusual originated by the far-from-tongue-tied insurance ace may be summed up in one word: "Impatience". There might a dozen other words more precisely fitting the case, but that one can fill the bill for now. Goodness knows, a generous helping of impatience was sorely needed in that complacent body.

Anyone seeing the "seven sages" in session over the past three or four years could well gather our meaning. Save for the weekly outbursts of George Nightingale - and those became such a part of the routine they went unnoticed - meetings of the City Fathers displayed one pervading quality - dullness. Routine topics provoked predictable comments, and were disposed of, either strictly by the book or amid gestures of futility - with least possible discussion. This item was referred to the Engineer. That one was contrary to the zoning regulations. Item 3 had been dealt with before and no solution was possible. It was too bad nothing could be done about item 4, but there simply isn't the money...And as for the last item, that wasn't the responsibility of Council: this is a job for Government, or private enterprise, or Superman.

And so the routine dodged along, imperturbable, serenely, and coldly impersonal. Follow the book, coddle the majority, don't waste time on the solitary individual and, this above all, don't drag out this meeting by coming up with any New Ideas! We haven't got time for that kind of nonsense...

Gordon Warren, rarely though he won the spotlight, came nearest in the outgoing administration to being a champion of the underdog. To him the rights of the individual were paramount, and steadfastly he upheld these rights, quietly and without an eye on headlines - as witness the few times he received them. Others won the spotlight, he said his simple piece and was done, letting human nature take its course. That nature, more often than not, proved all too human.

Warren's place has not been filled, and likely won't be. Idealism is out of fashion. That sense of fair play which was his unique contribution to city government must be left for his successors to emulate as best they can. The newcomers, however, have something a small bit different to offer. Of the two rookies, Alex Henley shows signs of having the more important part to play. No stranger to politics nor to public service, he brings to Council an asset which it has long lacked - an enquiring mind. A man of idealistic bent, though eminently practical, he's the sort who always wants to know why. Not so much "Why is this done?" - rather "Why can't this be done?. He carries a chip on his shoulder, a chip labelled "I want to be convinced."

Town Crier, and the NEWFOUNDLAND WEEKLY, did not prove convincing enough as, after putting up a valiant effort, the paper's lack of adequate advertising support put an end to its labours with its final edition Nov. 22nd, 1957.

5

Voice of the Common Man

VOCM IN THE 50S & 60S

When VOCM celebrated its 20th Anniversary in 1956, the station was beginning to climb the audience popularity charts to offer real competition for its five year old rival, CJON Radio. Making this possible was the cluster of strong broadcasting talent derived from a mixture of home grown and imported performers. Promotion of its top radio personalities was at the heart of advertising and marketing endeavours tied in with the anniversary celebrations.

Mengie Shulman, who had sparked significant upgrading of VOCM programming and entertainment values over the past decade was now moving into more of a background role. Stepping more and more into a leadership function was Denys Ferry, a radio professional from Owen Sound, Ontario, who took over as sales manager. Urbane, highly competent and intelligent, he was the station's principal news announcer, reading the news smoothly and effectively, sometimes with a theatrical touch. Not surprisingly because, settling permanently into St. John's life, he became deeply involved in amateur theatre in which he proved himself one of the city's finest actors.

Jim Regan, whose fine voice and good looks made him a favourite with many of the lady listeners, grew up in Halifax but his mother was from Cape Broyle. Jim's brother Gerald later became Premier of Nova Scotia and a federal cabinet minister.

Jim Murdock was a senior announcer when I first joined VOCM in 1953, and continued to serve for many years as one of the mainstays of the broadcasting staff, until his transfer to the new Grand Falls station.

Jim Browne's specialty was sports, as he wrote and read his own sportscasts, and did so for many years. He also moonlighted as a sports news contributor to the Evening Telegram.

Joining VOCM in the mid-50s, Bill Squires carved out a steady radio career there and in later years at CBC. In the half a dozen years when I worked with him, he ably handled a variety of announcing roles and proved a dab hand at writing witty commercials. A friendly, cheerful personality won him many friends. In the early '60s, when Harold Butler left VOCM to become manager of a new radio station, CFCB, in Corner Brook, Bill went out with him to help put it on the air. He stayed at CFCB, an independent station owned by Dr. Noel Murphy of Corner Brook, until 1962. In July of that year, he headed for Marystown to provide a similar service for the new outlet, CHCM, managed by Charlie Noseworthy. Six months later he helped Jim Murdock to put the new station CKCM on the air in Grand Falls, and remained there "as his sidekick" for two years. Over the next three years, Bill tried his luck at mainland stations ranging from Yarmouth, N.S., to British Columbia. He wound up his broadcasting career with a 14-year stint at CBC in St. John's as an announcer and later as a producer.

When Omar Blondahl arrived at VOCM to commence his flamboyant career as folk singing Sagebrush Sam, he and Bill became the best of friends, and they often teamed up on special appearances around the island.

One such venture in the fall of 1956, as Bill recalls, was rather different:

> Omar and I were having a beer at our favourite watering hole, the bar of the Newfoundland Hotel, when we were interrupted by a gruff-voiced gentleman who introduced himself as Senator Bill Petten. He was in town, he said, to assist Joe Smallwood with the provincial election which was slated the following month. "B'ys," he said, "the Premier wants to see ya." To which we replied "Sure, and I suppose the Queen wants to see us after that."
>
> "No," he said, "I'm serious. Come on, I'll drive you to his office." The office was at Fort Townshend. So away we went. Joey greeted us in his inimitable manner and revealed that he wanted us to assist in the election in the St. Shott's area, for which he handed us $500 each with the promise of another five hundred after the election. Naturally Omar and I jumped at it, and the next day we joined up with the Myles Murray campaign

which was led by none other than our old friend, Greg O'Grady of IOCC fame.

We arrived at St. Shott's next day and headed for the parish hall, only to discover that our trip and good intentions were in vain. We had about 10 pieces of equipment - microphones, speakers, turntables, etc. - guess what? They had no electricity, nor would they have any for another 10 or more years. The show per se did not go on, although Omar did a few songs without the aid of a mike. And I was a dead loss because I couldn't perform as I needed a turntable and speaker for my lip-sync performance - we called it pantomime in those days. Needless to say, we didn't hear from Joey after. You'd think someone would have forewarned us, eh!

Bill and Omar and I palled around quite a bit that year, enjoying our share of beer talk at various watering holes within easy reach of the station. I fondly recall sitting in a VOCM control booth one evening, watching as they both improvised sound effects for a demo tape of the folk song "John Hinks" that Omar was recording for Rodeo Records. The write-up I did of Omar's singing career was fun to do for such a friendly and interesting individual. One small regret from those days - I was supposed to go along with Omar and Bill for that trip to Maher's when they effected that rescue of 'Charlie Horse' from Angle Pond. Something to do with a date I couldn't pass up. Had I gone, I might have been immortalized in that famous song.

Bound for Glory

Two young home grown recruits - Bob Cole and Harry Brown - earned at VOCM in that period much of the broadcasting skills and finesse that led them to national prominence or better in later years. I knew them both in school days - Bob as a young Feildians hockey player and Harry as older brother of Bill Brown, one of my best friends at St. Bon's. Harry was also a former hockey team mate of mine at St. Bon's and Memorial.

Bob Cole started as an announcer at VOCM in 1956 after deciding against getting into an airline flying career. He stayed for six years before moving on to CBC in St. John's. His love for hockey showed up early in his VOCM days, as he liked to huddle with a tape recorder, practising the play by play skills that were to launch his phenomenal career as the next Foster Hewitt. He covered his first Stanley Cup game in 1969. Oddly enough, one of his predecessors as a VOCM play by play specialist was Don Jamieson, years before CJON came into being. I remember Don broadcasting some of our inter-collegiate hockey games in the latter 1940s at the old St. Bon's Forum.

Bob was inducted in 1996 into the Hockey Hall of Fame and won the Foster Hewitt Memorial Award for excellence in hockey broadcasting. He's still doing the Stanley Cup playoffs. Despite his incredible travel schedule with the NHL, he has kept his home and family in Newfoundland. As he says, it's only 15 minutes to the airport.

Harry Brown had first worked in radio in 1951 at CJON where he did, among other things, hosting for an afternoon Kiddies Carnival show, styling himself as Uncle Harry. Moving to VOCM a few years later, he carried this persona with him, hosting a successful young talent show which launched the careers of several outstanding performers, notably pop singer Mary Lou Collins. Harry got into radio after spending a few years in the Air Force. He left VOCM, rather suddenly, in 1957, explaining to friends later how this happened.

An exuberant personality with a lively sense of humour, he ran afoul of management while kibitzing with a technician buddy, Gordon Tizzard with whom he routinely exchanged greetings by reversing the pronunciation of each other's first name. Reacting to a friendly but unexpected lunge from his partner, and unaware that he was sitting in front of an open mike, Harry burst out "Oh Jesus, Nodrog!". Management, needless to say, especially in view of the owner's religious leanings, were not amused, and he was fired forthwith.

Soon finding a soft landing at CBC, he settled down to a successful career, transferring in 1968 to Toronto where he co-hosted such high profile programs as As It Happens with Barbara Frum. I always thought Harry did a better job than she did, but she got all the plaudits. I visited Harry one afternoon at CBC's Jarvis Street studios while he was taping segments of that evening's As It Happens show. We had a good chat about old times and new, in between his long distance phone interviews on any number of subjects.

Another local who made it big was Owen Godden whom Dave Maunder remembers as arriving at VOCM as a school kid in short pants. He hung around the station until being offered a job. His deep resonant voice assured him of a future in news broadcasting, and he did eventually land in Toronto with CBC, but apparently died rather young. Summer replacements for on-air staff included Rick Cashin who, though not set on any broadcasting career, did make a name for himself in the political arena and in the unlikely realm of fisheries unionism. He won election to Parliament in 1962 and in later years served as President of the Newfoundland Fishermen, Food and Allied Workers Union. Technical staff throughout the period included Charlie Noseworthy (before he was transferred to Marystown as station manager), Gordon Tizzard and Dave Maunder.

Other Imports

There was considerable reliance on imported talent to handle announcer duties at VOCM in the 1950s. Among these was one American, Ed Flynn, who had been stationed at Pepperrell Air Force Base and had done on air programs on the base radio station. He was a keen admirer of the music of Frank Sinatra and other "standards" in his choice of musical selections. I once had the opportunity to introduce him to a St. John's friend of mine who had the same name. The latter Ed Flynn couldn't have been more different. An intellectual who became a professor of English at St. Mary's University in Halifax, he much preferred jazz.

Bob Lockhart, who came to VOCM as a staff announcer from his native New Brunswick around 1957 was one of the more flamboyant characters with whom I worked. A lively and genial individual, he was a popular on air personality and got actively involved in various community activities. Spending many of his off hours in scuba diving, he teamed up with Derm Dobbin in several daring exploits endeavouring to rescue children trapped underwater in spring flooding accidents. He and his wife Betty were also socially active.

Bob's interests extended increasingly into news work and he developed freelance correspondent arrangements with a number of mainland media. In later years he returned to New Brunswick, becoming managing director of CFBC and branching into the cable industry. Always interested in politics, he served a number of terms as Mayor of Saint John N.B. Bob was also very active in the armed forces reserve - an avocation that gained him some interesting assignments in later years. I ran into him once just after he had completed a fairly lengthy assignment with the Canadian peace keeping force on Cyprus. He also reportedly worked as a photojournalist in such diverse arenas as Viet Nam, Bosnia. Kosovo and Afghanistan. At last report, he had retired from broadcasting, and from the army reserve, where he had attained the rank of lieutenant-colonel, and was completing his doctoral thesis at the University of New Brunswick in Fredericton.

Bill Allen was a Montreal broadcaster who became a popular VOCM staffer for several years. His actual name was Bill Jameson, but the "Allen" surname was chosen to ensure he was not mistaken for one of the Jamieson clan at CJON.

Merv Russell, an announcer from Saint John, NB was also a well known VOCM staffer for some time. He later moved on to CJON and got involved in politics, running for the PC Party in St. John East Extern. He lost out, and returned to the mainland. In recent years, he served as President of Maritime Broadcasting Systems Ltd. In Halifax. He also worked closely with entrepreneur Harry Steele at Eastern Provincial Airways and in his other endeavours.

By the time that VOCM marked its 30th anniversary in 1966, operations had expanded significantly. The Colonial Broadcasting System, as it was called, added in 1962 a second station, CKCM, operating on 10,000 watts at Grand Falls, and a smaller station, CHCM, operating on 1,000 watts at Marystown. Joseph V. Butler, second son of VOCM's founder, took over as President and Managing Director in 1961. His older brother, Harold, moved to Corner Brook as manager of a new station, CFCB.

NEWFOUNDLAND NIGHT

My last encounter with Harry Brown was a memorable one, when he accepted my invitation to emcee a special Newfoundland Night at the National Press Club in Ottawa. This was a gala affair, held October 28, 1983, to mark the 400th anniversary of Newfoundland's founding as Britain's oldest colony. Then co-host of CBC-TV's popular show Take 30, Harry's prowess as a Master of Ceremonies for such events was widely known. Promotional efforts paid off when some 150 communications and political figures crowded into the Press Club dining room to feast on Newfoundland delicacies and culture. Sold out ten days in advance, it could have taken in 150 more. Prominent attendees, in addition to the guest speakers, included Senators Jack Marshall and Bill Petten, Fisheries and Oceans Deputy Minister, Dr. Art May, and former deputy Don Tansley.

Heading up the organizing committee, I got wonderful support and cooperation from government and business organizations in Newfoundland. Len Simms, Minister of Culture, Recreation and Youth, made a special trip to Ottawa for the occasion. A veritable smorgasbord of Newfoundland seafood, from sole, flounder and shrimp to cod tongues, plus a bakeapple dessert, was prepared and served by the Press Club's celebrated chef Peter Adelberg, based largely on advice from Cathy O'Brien, consumer consultant with the federal Fisheries and Oceans department in St. John's, who also came for the dinner. All seafood supplies were provided free of charge by member firms of the Fisheries Association of Newfoundland, while donations of Dominion Ale from Carling O'Keefe and Newman's Port wine from Watley's Ltd. added uniquely to audience enjoyment.

Special entertainment was provided by "The Barkin' Kettle", a quintet of talented traditional Newfoundland musicians - Marilyn Benson, Jean Hewson, Brian Murphy, Wanda Crocker and Lindsay Hartery - who were flown in gratis with the compliments of Eastern Provincial Airways President Harry Steele. Looking after the musicians proved a mixture of pain and pleasure for me, having to book a van to pick up and deliver bulky sound equipment for them, but relaxing with them over a few pre-dinner drinks in a nearby pub.

Speakers, including Conservative Culture Minister Len Simms, Liberal M.P. Rogers Simmons, and Senator Bill Doody (a former classmate of mine) for the most part kept their remarks brief and light hearted in tone. Max Keeping, reigning then and now as the best known TV news personality in Ottawa, as News Director of CJOH TV, responded in kind to a toast to the media. He confided to me later that this didn't come easy for him this time because Harry Brown was such a hard act to follow.

Harry, indeed, was far and away the star performer of the evening. His remarks, anything but brief, celebrated and exemplified the Newfoundland character with an incredibly hilarious and exhaustive succession of jokes and expressions and stories. The audience, less than one quarter of whom were Newfoundlanders. loved every minute of it until the midnight hour. A note received later from CJOH confirmed that Max Keeping had a great time - he and Harry ended up together closing the bar.

A Newman's Port wine bottle label sits in my souvenir file as a poignant remembrance of a remarkable event, and a most remarkable individual. It bears this imprint:

Bottled especially for

Harry Brown

UPS AND DOWNS AT VOCM NEWS

It's always nice to get a second chance to do something you believe in, and that's how I felt when I walked into VOCM soon after New Year's 1957. Nearly three years earlier, I had been the station's first staff news reporter, but the experiment fizzled out after four months of solitary frustration. My dream of developing an effective news reporting service had then to be put on hold.

Working with Harvey's News Bulletin since the fall of 1954 had kept me necessarily in close touch with VOCM, and increasingly rekindled my conviction that any news carried on the station should surely be produced at and by the station. The common sense of this view at last gained recognition by both parties, so agreement was reached for me and my colleague Jack Howlett to be transferred from Harvey and Company at the start of 1957. We would still be producing Harvey's News, but other newscasts throughout the day as well.

That was a busy but enjoyable experience as we tinkered with newscast time slots and explored ways of improving and expanding news sources and resources. Useful staff help came aboard in the person of experienced sports reporter and personality Noel Vinnicombe, and Bob Moss, a keen but initially unpromising new recruit. Noel had proved himself a very able and productive news gatherer, partly because of his extensive contacts throughout the city due to his prominence in sports and his friendly and gregarious personality. VOCM staff announcers were mainly friendly and cooperative, and before long a genuinely productive newsroom operation got into full swing. Working with our small news team, however, suffered a disappointing setback when, within a few months of my arrival, station management suddenly laid off Noel Vinnicombe. They did so without giving me, or anyone else, any advance warning or explanation.

Still the work carried on. Producing the major newscasts took top priority, but we got as much local news as possible into hourly 5-minute newscasts. These were aired five minutes before the hour - a ploy to upstage the much ballyhooed "First With the News in Newfoundland" boast of our chief rival, CJON, which aired its newscasts every hour on the hour. Filling five minutes of air time with news every hour was no easy task for this fledgling group so we relied perforce on a fair amount of newswire copy. Early on, we had two wire services feeding us copy - Broadcast News provided by the Canadian

Press, and British United Press. "Rip and read" copy was ever useful, but we made sure local news came first and foremost unless something earthshaking had happened elsewhere.

Because VOCM had no history of gathering news on its own, building up of a network of correspondents across the province was an immediate priority. Having dealt directly with some regular correspondents at Harvey's News, I engaged them right away as VOCM correspondents. The best and most prolific of them all was Fred Tessier of Grand Bank, a businessman who served as Mayor of the town for years, and had his finger into everything going in that community. His reports, sent by telegram, were always timely, thorough and well written, rarely requiring any rewriting for broadcast use.

Other correspondents were heard from fairly regularly on happenings at centres such as Bell Island, Harbour Grace, Argentia and Bonavista. A frequent contributor from Bell Island was Steve Neary, then a prominent mining union leader. Another labour union head, Esau Thoms, covered community as well as union news from Argentia. One correspondent, whom I never met though I have seen his name from time to time over the years, was Francis Patey of St. Anthony, one of my early recruits. Getting to know and hear from these faithful chroniclers of community activities proved one of the more satisfying experiences of that era. Another regularly heard from was Joshua Stansford from Grate's Cove, who faithfully recorded doings large and small in and around that small fishing village at the tip of the peninsula separating Conception and Trinity Bays. He left for posterity a book "Fifty Years of My Life in Nfld", recording in large part the ups and downs of weather variations in that period. Injection of stories from these coastal correspondents added a saving touch of humanity to the daily catalogue of traffic and marine accidents, criminal cases, political skirmishing and catastrophe that made up the bulk of news content aired for public consumption.

My reporting routine continued to focus on coverage of the major news beats of the capital, including weekly meetings of the St. John's city council, House of Assembly sessions when the house was open, any significant Supreme Court and Magistrate's Court cases, and "press" conferences by politicians and business leaders. City Hall and the courts were within walking distance from the McBride's Hill VOCM studios, but I needed my car to go to the House of Assembly, then located in the old Colonial Building on Military Road.

While the early months at VOCM were very busy but enjoyable, circumstances took a turn for the worse when Jack Howlett, my highly competent and personable partner from Harvey's News, accepted a job as a news editor with our deadly rival, CJON. I tried in vain to persuade VOCM management - then under direction of Harold N. "Sonny" Butler - to give him a raise that might have persuaded him to stay. Coming as it did not long after losing Noel Vinnicombe, it left me up a big creek without a paddle.

Then followed what was for me an ever greater calamity - I was informed that management in its wisdom was bringing the newsroom up to strength by transferring two other staff members to help us out. The two - elderly accountant Fred Ruggles Sr. and a young school friend of one of the Butler brothers, Roy Pike. Neither had the slightest experience or aptitude for news work, but all of my protestations met a deaf ear, and I had no choice but to put up with such arbitrary treatment. I was still at this time far from satisfied with the skills of my only remaining staffer, Bob Moss, so I just gritted my teeth and resolved to make the best of a bad lot. Covering the top news of the times was my main preoccupation, and this at least sustained me throughout the period.

As time went on, I learned to reassess my judgment about Bob Moss whom, through my initial dealings with him, I had caustically dismissed as "the rolling Moss who gathers no news". This was an unkind, and highly politically incorrect, reference to his ambling gait due, if I recall correctly, to a onetime leg injury. Bob, in fact, developed later into a highly effective news "digger", sniffing out news stories that others couldn't see. He became a constant burr in the side of unwary politicians and business leaders who mistook his outharbour manner of speaking for lack of intelligence. He had no fear of the high and mighty, and doggedly pursued the substance of a story with admirable passion and conviction. Bob and I indeed became the best of friends and I followed with interest his career path from radio to the newspaper world as Editor for many years of the Gander Beacon. In those dark VOCM days in 1957, however, his light had yet to break the surface.

Old Mr. Ruggles, as I thought of him, was always apologetic for being thrust upon me in this way, and obligingly took on a thankless chore in compiling a reference file of ongoing news events for use in backgrounding future stories. It gave him something to do on a project I had tried to initiate, but it didn't make filling the hourly newscasts any easier.

My frustrations with VOCM management spilled over that fall when I rather hastily decided to quit after being refused a hoped for increase in salary. I had been told that a salary review would be made after my first six months on the job, but heard nothing and raised the question with managing director Harold Butler one October morning, again to no avail. Stomping out of his office, I dashed off a letter of resignation saying, in part:

> The explanation give by you, namely that a re-appraisal of jobs scheduled for March next made it impossible to grant any salary increases, was both misleading and insulting. I must thank your brother (Joe Butler) for having the honesty to state your real reasons. I was told by him that there has not been sufficient improvement in the newsroom to warrant a raise in salary for me. He mentioned errors of other Newsroom staff, my own unpunctuality in arriving for work in the morning, and an absence of improvement in the general quality of the News.

I pointed out that improvement in performance could not be expected without fully competent staff. As for morning tardiness, I suggested that this was made up for by working half way through lunch hour and until 6.45 (news time) each evening. And I cited my Harvey's boss, Ray Simmons's contention that "a newsman is an artist" and providing he gets results, the actual hours he works are not really important. I did suggest that in this regard I was "like, wine, improving with age."

Bringing Ray Simmons' name into it probably helped. Indeed, Ray was quick to back me up in later discussion with the Butlers and, after some negotiation, my resignation was withdrawn. I thus carried on with the job, a little mollified by the recognition, implicit if unspoken, that my words of protest were amply warranted. And I did eventually get a raise, albeit a modest one - from $3,730 in 1957 to $4,180 in 1958.

I suspect Ray Simmons' influence came to my rescue on another occasion during my tenure at VOCM. Well do I remember the afternoon I walked into the legislative chamber in the House of Assembly, ready for coverage of Question Period and other business to follow, only to find no room for me in the press section. In the Colonial Building, where the House met until transferring to the Confederation Building in 1960, there were about a dozen press table seats facing the

Assembly chamber, and I as a regular reporter occupied one of these seats. This time, however, all of the spaces were taken.

This afternoon, Premier Smallwood was due to make a special announcement - something to do with a major Education study, I think it was - one in a series of big announcements of supposedly mammoth importance to the well being of the province. To underline the significance of the occasion, our news rivals on the hill (Prince of Wales St.) had come early and installed, amid the Press Table seats, a huge mounted TV camera. I remonstrated vociferously at this unprecedented intrusion of TV equipment in an area reserved for news reporters only. The TV people refused to budge, so I was left to fume outside as the camera whirled and everyone else clutched the proffered announcement handout, noting down the comments of government and opposition representatives.

That evening's Harvey's News Bulletin report on the House of Assembly was conspicuously lacking in detailed coverage of the great announcement. In fact, there was just the barest mention of the fact that the Premier had announced a new Education policy - or whatever it was. But no more than that.

Well, did the fat ever hit the fan the next day! VOCM's station manager got a zinger from Sir Leonard Outerbridge, the Lieutenant Governor (whose family were major Harvey and Company directors). Sir Leonard had received a blast from the Premier. Ultimately, of course, I was called on the carpet. Why didn't we have the big announcement on the news? I had my answer all ready: Because I couldn't get into the Press Table. I couldn't get the announcement, so I had nothing to report. Blame it on CJON!

Visions of getting fired danced through my head for hours after that, but somehow, if any bullets were flying, I dodged them all. I know, everyone told me I was being foolish and stubborn by taking this boycott tack, but I just couldn't let this one pass. I did get my ears burned and my judgment scolded, but the storm blew over. I do know Ray Simmons spoke up boldly in my defence and he had enough credit with the upper echelons to gain me yet another reprieve. I thank him for that. The TV cameras never showed up again in that Press Table area.

Keeping up with the doings of politicians is an important part of the news reporting game, so it's always helpful to have the politicians feeding in timely reports for use whenever appropriate. This is especially desirable for radio broadcast, particularly for letting people know when and where the member is going to be for meetings with constituents. One of the most faithful sources of this kind of information was Charlie Granger who served from 1953 to 1957 as executive assistant to federal cabinet minister Jack Pickersgill. As Newfoundland's representative in the cabinet, Pickersgill was a frequent visitor to the province from Ottawa and worked very closely with Premier Smallwood.

Every time Pickersgill came to Newfoundland, Granger made sure to notify all newsrooms in the area about the Minister's itinerary, with some details about his plans for the visit. All very fine, and we newsroom people would be only too happy to fit this information into our newscasts. This was all the more welcome because Charlie was a good writer and his reports could well be used with minimal editing.

But there was one thing that rankled me once too often about Charlie's Ottawa reports. They always came in by telegram collect. In those days, sending information by telegram was still in common use, especially for long distance communications. However, telegrams arriving with news for radio stations were rarely sent collect and, if any were received, they would usually be ignored.

Not so when they divulged the activities of our only minister in Canada's cabinet.

Well, one day, when fretting about this casual imposition on our good will, I threw caution to the winds and led off the next newscast with an item reading somewhat like this:

> Newfoundland's representative in the federal Cabinet,
> J.W. Pickersgill, will be visiting his Bonavista-Twillingate
> riding this weekend. The Minister advised VOCM by
> collect telegram today that the visit will cover four days
> and include meetings in Bonavista and Catalina as well
> as his summer residence in the Port Blandford area...

No angry phone calls surfaced right away but a day or so later I did hear from Charlie Granger, asking if it was true that the expression "collect telegram" had been used in our report on this visit. I admitted that something of that kind had slipped through somehow. Neither of us made any issue of it. I was just content that he did get the message, while Charlie, whom I always found to be a really nice and considerate man, was too polite to make any fuss about it.

Not that it mattered really. The collect telegrams continued to come in anyway.

No Room at the Inn

Harvey's News story (Jan. 1958) read, in best theatrical style, by the incomparable Denys Ferry:

> Here's a story we got straight from the horse's mouth.
>
> It seems a city businessman was carrying out a rather extended New Year's celebration, whirling about the countryside with a horse and sleigh. Running short of private supplies of the Christmas spirit, he decided about ten o'clock last evening to drop in at a suburban night club. Cantering up to the door, the horse stopped and the passengers got off. But the master of ceremonies, and of the horse, felt it would be highly ungrateful of him to leave his trusty steed high and dry at the doorstep, so he undertook to drag horse, sleigh and all into the club with him.
>
> Perhaps he thought this club was one bearing the name of a well-known beverage; it might be that he decided to donate some horse meat to the kitchen; or - who knows? - he may have been just one of those people who take the stand: "Anywhere I go, my horse goes with me." Whatever his motives, he pulled on the reins, and began leading the animal in through the doorway.
>
> Meanwhile, the club manager, hearing these rather unfamiliar steps at the threshold, came to the door to inform his latest guest that hob-nailed boots were not permitted on the dance floor. Greeted by the sight of the head and shoulders of our friend Dobbin, the startled manager began to remonstrate with its owner, insisting that while the club could overlook the absence of white shirt and tie, it had to draw the line somewhere: "Really, you know, one must wear a top-coat!"
>
> At this point, some other patrons were trying to gain admittance, and forthwith a tug-o'-war ensued, the newcomers pulling back the sleigh, and the self-appointed agent of the SPCA tugging on the reins in the

opposite direction. Eventually, however, the manager's arguments won out, and the horse and sleigh retreated.

Unfortunately, the matter was not to end there. Failing to establish the right of his steed to go in for a beer, the frustrated owner found that he himself was not to be served either. Brushing aside the objection that he had had more than enough already, he demanded service. Argument was resumed but was not effective. Suddenly a fist shot out, and the club manager found himself heaped in a corner. Then a kick struck him in the face, just before employees ran to his assistance.

Though no more fisticuffs ensued, the assailant was unceremoniously dumped outside the door, warned never to come back again, and warned further that "This wasn't the last he'd hear of this incident."

And with this, activities at the club finally returned to normal.

This story was come by honestly, since I saw the whole thing from an upstairs table overlooking the entrance. The incident took place at the Old Mill, a very popular night club located on Brookfield Road near Ruby Line. Gerry Stephens, an enigmatic individual of German background who ran the club very successfully for a number of years, was the embattled club manager. As for the horseman, it may best be said that he and his sleigh companion were rather well known in gossipy circles for their unconventional lifestyle.

YEAR OF THE BEARDS

1958 was a landmark year for VOCM as the station leaped into broadcasting's big leagues by boosting its power from a mere 1,000 to 10,000 watts. Celebrations to mark the event were generated with maximum publicity, highlighted by a beard growing challenge flung across the continent to British Columbia. Twelve VOCM staffers, myself included, signed a solemn pact in July to refrain from shaving at least until power boosting day, September 1st. The VOCM challenge was accepted by a Cranbrook, B.C. radio station, CKEK, whose beard growers pledged to continued unshaven until the end of the year. For British Columbians, beard-growing had already been embraced as one way to celebrate that province's centennial.

News of the trans-Canada contest gained national as well as provincial attention. The national trade magazine "Broadcaster and Telescreen" featured the event in its August issue with "The Shaggy Men Story". Launching of VOCM's challenge threatened participants who broke their pact with forfeiture of a $5 payment to the St. John's playground association. Plans were to award the local contest prize, when the station went to full power, to the staffer who grew 10,000 or more whiskers. Just how the counting was to be done was never clearly outlined.

While B.C. and Newfoundland radio folk got into the spirit of shirking off shaving, one of our neighbours to the south got into trouble for suggesting a similar stunt. The Junior Chamber of Commerce in Vernon, Connecticut, proposed a beard growing contest for that community's 150th anniversary celebrations. Then it abandoned the idea. Too many people said their employers threatened to fire them if they grew beards.

Ticklish as it could be, beard growing proved a popular pastime for participants and onlookers alike, and everyone had a lot of fun observing how suavely or scruffily individuals went about grooming their growth. Publicity photos recorded periodically the pace of whisker advancement, quite variable from one competitor to another as it turned out. While an even dozen reportedly initialled the no shaving pledge, only 10 showed up on an early publicity photo. My favourite PR shot has me (the gap-toothed one) and Bill Squires cuddling up to our most attractive colleague, Mary Hollett, with mellow toned Ed Flynn with eyes half closed behind us. Ultimate winner, if I rightly remember it, was Edgar Squires, but some among us suggested they liked mine best. I know I did, though Madeline, my long suffering fiancée, was not nearly so impressed. "It's like kissing a box of shredded wheat", she opined to anyone who asked.

Cranking out publicity items on the power boosting beard contest enlivened many an otherwise mishap and mayhem-filled newscast. How else to work into an everyday news report the revelation that Roman senator Cicero considered beards, albeit somewhat ornamental, were really of no use at all? Other nuggets of debatable wisdom on beard growing practice were freely offered:

The poet, Lord Byron, for example, took it for granted that before Adam and Eve were banished from Paradise, Adam had no beard. And Byron says

That ever since the fall, man for his sin,

Has had a beard entailed upon his chin.

Voltaire, the French philosopher, had his own cynical way of looking at the custom. Ideas, he said, were like beards - "Children and women never have them." ...

Some of the ancient writers took a dim view of men growing long beards, but others believed it was what Newfoundlanders call 'the proper t'ing.' Thus one author declares that "it is clear woman was intended to be smooth and silly, exalting naturally in her hair alone, but man was adorned with a beard like a lion, making him tough, with a hairy chest, for such is the symbol of strength and empire."

...

But here's another fellow who comes right out and has his say on the burning question...

The beard, says he, is an aggressive portent of male domination. Did our Victorian forefathers trouble their minds over women's rights? They did not, says he. Their beards were the answer to all such flapdoodle and finookery.

Hmm. Flapdoodle and finookery. Now there are two good words indeed. Must remember them the next time the wife spends all the grocery money on a new sack dress.

Shades of yesteryear! Imagine trying to air such weighty sentiments in this enlightened age! And what may I ask is a sack dress?

Just how the VOCM challengers fared as against the Cranbrookers out west may have gotten lost in the mists of time, but chances are that no one really bothered to keep score. By power boosting time, however, the VOCM beard promotion had proved its worth, and audience growth rose with it.

A few of us stayed bearded well into the following year - in my case until shortly before my days of easeful bachelorhood came to an end, as Madeline and I (clean shaven at last) got married in June.

6

The News Fraternity

ST. PIERRE WITH EPA

The organization of press tours to promote media and public awareness of important activities and innovations was a welcome development in the late 1950s.

On a sunny day in June 1958, Eastern Provincial Airways inaugurated a new passenger service from St. John's to St. Pierre with a special flight for invited press, radio and television representatives. An enjoyable time was had by all. The service, using a 28-passenger DC-3 aircraft, extended also from St. Pierre to Sydney, N.S., but we did the first link only. With a population at that time of 5,000, the French islands of St. Pierre and Miquelon lie only 25 kilometres off the southernmost tip of the Burin peninsula. 4,000 resided in the town of St. Pierre, the commercial centre of the colony.

On our arrival at St. Pierre, the group was treated to a reception and luncheon, followed by a tour of the rather brief island road system. Afterwards, there was time to explore some of the island's shops and eateries.

A Nfld. Journal of Commerce report published following the media visit aptly described two of the island's notable phenomena - the popularity of wine and its chaotic motor traffic:

> Fresh water is scarce at St. Pierre and is used primarily for ablution rather than as a beverage. Wine is served with all meals, French style, and lovers of cognac will find the best procurable at St. Pierre. This also applies to the table wines and the champagne.
> Most of the automobiles on the islands are of French manufacture and taxis, cheap, just blow their way

through the narrow twisting streets and around blind corners. There appear to be no traffic regulations. The horn, rather than any specified rule of the road, makes the road clear for the driver.

Well, but not without a grimace, do I remember that St. Pierre champagne. We lapped it up unwisely and until the wee hours in a Saturday night revel at one of the big dance halls. Next morning, faithfully turning out for Sunday Mass in a service punctuated with innumerable sequences of standing, sitting, kneeling and standing up again, the head was reeling unmercifully. Jamais, jamais plus!

Interesting sites that we took in on our short but enjoyable visit included the St. Pierre graveyard, noted for its above ground burial vaults. Another inevitable centre of attention on this small but intriguing outpost of France in the northwest Atlantic was the St. Pierre waterfront. The flag-bedecked vessel at dockside aroused some curiosity, but memory fails in regard to the occasion - could it have been for Bastille Day?

On our departure, members of the group clutched packages of souvenirs, mainly of the liquid variety so amply and cheaply sold everywhere on the island.

Saddest expression of the day was that of Ian Macdonald who inadvertently let his package slip and crash upon the solid airport tarmac, splintering into a thousand pieces. His friends offered what consolation they could from champagne intended for home consumption. There were headaches all around next day to remind travellers of a unique break from their regular news coverage routine.

NEWFOUNDLAND PRESS CLUB

From my earliest days as a radio news reporter, I enjoyed meeting and talking shop with other news people, and joined in any activities which brought members of the news fraternity together. An always enjoyable venue for so doing was an occasional meeting of the Newfoundland Press Club. As early as the fall of 1953, while I was in my first stint working at VOCM, I went to one or two meetings of the club held in the Press Room of the House of Assembly, then located in the former Colonial Building on Military Road. Meetings were quite informal and leaned more toward socializing than serious business, which suited all concerned.

One noteworthy gathering which I attended at the Press Room was an informal presentation to Art Pratt with whom I had many pleasant moments when I was working nights at the Daily News. He had since become Night Editor at the News but was now about to embark on a new career in the heady precincts of public relations. Held in high esteem by his press and radio colleagues, he was leaving the next day for Montreal to begin his public relations duties with Canadian National Railways. Members of the Newfoundland Press Club took this occasion to honour him as Past President of the club.

Other locales than the legislative Press Room were used for an occasional festive occasion. One quite successful event took place on Topsail Road at Barney's, probably the most popular out of town eatery in the area. Until, that is, the next day, when it burned to the ground. Nobody blamed us, fortunately.

Press Club gatherings bred a healthful camaraderie among news people despite keen rivalries among the various print, radio and, as of 1955, television media. Occasional squabbles about access to ministers and hard to get government information were usually resolved by joint representations in the club's name. Activities, for the most part however, involved pleasurable get-togethers, including open house (free beer) parties at local breweries. Most news types liked to quaff an ale or two in those far off days when PC was a party label, not a certificate of political correctness.

One of my more memorable, though briefly painful, such events was the Annual Press Club Dinner held Sunday, April 22nd 1956 at Gerry Byrne's popular hostelry at Donovans on the Topsail highway. As recorded in a newspaper report, it was described as an outstanding success with some 25 members of the press and radio attending. They included Acting club President George Perlin, Secretary Harold Horwood, Treasurer Mark Ronayne, Dave Butler, Gerry Bowering, Dave Gilbert, Harvey Clarke, Arch Sullivan, Nelson Squires, Dick Squires, Lloyd Sheppard, Leo Shea, Jim Regan, Doug Brophy, John Holmes, Nix Wadden, Aubrey Mack, Noel Vinnicombe, Bill Werthman, Don Morris and Jack Howlett. Club President that year had been Art Pratt of the Daily News, but he had resigned to accept a job with the public relations department of Canadian National Railways in Moncton, N.B.

My painful experience on that occasion occurred when, in rising from the table, I slipped and, to my utmost embarrassment, banged my head on the floor. My consumption of beer, though not drastically in excess, no doubt contributed to the mishap, and I was not soon to be allowed to forget it.

Next day, an envelope appeared on my desk at Harvey's News with a cartoon enclosure. I might have known - the sender identifying himself with a head shot was Daily News photographer Dave Butler. Dave, who a year or two later moved away for a federal government communications job, ended up as boss of a flourishing communications firm, Marshall Fenn, with which I did some business years later when I too had moved on from media news to a career in federal government PR.

Press Club Revival

Ironically, following the success of the 1956 annual dinner, the Press Club went through a period of inactivity which lasted for two years. Toward the end of that period, a desire for club revival was rekindled, particularly among reporters assembling in an unlikely mileu. The Federal Civil Servants Club, located on Duckworth Street, was, despite its official sounding name, a friendly and informal watering hole for members and guests alike. Manager throughout that period was Vince Rossiter, with whom I renewed acquaintance decades later when I too was a federal employee and we both worked with the Fisheries Department in Ottawa.

We in the media were welcomed and granted associate club membership which meant, of course, that we could use the bar and play darts, a popular pastime there and in most of the taverns and clubs around the city. Given that the club was walking distance away from both newspapers, the News and the Telegram and two radio stations - VOCM and CBC, as well as the courts and city hall (then also on Duckworth Street), it was a handy and comfortable milieu for swapping stories and sharing observations on the follies of our employers, our politicians, and life in general. Which means we had a lot of fun.

Around the club tables, it was guy talk usually, as we had very few news women in that era - indeed "newsman" was the common term for anyone in the reporting trade. One of the few women reporters among us, Pat Lees of the Daily News, acted and was readily treated as "one of the boys", despite the disadvantage of an unmistakable English accent. Many a lively discussion in that heady atmosphere laid the groundwork for the drive to organize a new and highly activist Press Club to serve both our journalistic and social needs.

By the summer of 1958, interest in and enthusiasm for reviving the Press Club reached peak level, and action was taken, as recorded in this July 10 press report:

> Representatives from all the St. John's news media unanimously voted last night to reactivate the Newfoundland Press Club - an organization of men and women directly concerned with the gathering, compilation and presentation of news. The old Press Club disbanded about two years ago and many members felt that it should be brought back into being. Spearheading the efforts lately have been Nix Wadden of Radio Station VOCM and Bruce Woodland of the Fisheries Department who called a meeting last night in the clubrooms of the Civil Servants Association who kindly lent their premises for the Press Club's meeting. Following a general discussion of what the new Press Club should be, an election of officers was held and Mr. Wadden was elected president by acclamation. Mrs. Pat Lees is the vice-president, Tony Thomas the secretary and Charlie Bursey the treasurer. The executive will hold a meeting early next week to draw up a constitution and to detail activities of the club. Tentatively, meetings of the membership will be the first Wednesday of each month but the executive will call another general meeting soon after completing the constitution. Among some of the points brought up at last night's meeting were a suggestion that news representatives in other

Newfoundland communities be asked to join the Club, an effort to draw up resolutions to raise the standards of news reporting and a hope that visiting newsmen will visit the local Club to meet Newfoundland newsmen.

Considerable club activity was undertaken that fall and winter, sometimes on a monthly basis, as the club took upon itself to organize both professional and social events.

Of the colleagues putting in so much work on that club executive, Tony Thomas was my closest and most dedicated companion in these endeavours, and we became the best of friends. He was also a first rate newsman, well known and well respected for his journalistic prowess and his high level of service to the fourth estate community. He worked for many years as a stalwart of the Evening Telegram news staff. Later on he graduated into a public relations and communications career, first in private business and then with a federal government department.

Nfld. Press Club Executive elected July 1958 are (l-r):- Tony Thomas, Telegram (Secretary); Charlie Bursey, Doyle Bulletin (Treasurer); Nix Wadden, VOCM (President)

PRESS CLUB TOURS

A significant innovation by the Press Club in 1958 was the organization of the club's own press tours of major military and mining sites in the province. One group gained an invitation to pay a visit to the United States Naval Station in Argentia. I did not make that trip, but joined a larger group which later on made a well organized tour of the United States Air Force Base in Stephenville - Harmon Air Force Base as it was called.

The United States set up a number of military bases in Newfoundland during the Second World War to help in the protection of North America in those turbulent times. They were an important part of the celebrated lend lease agreement reached between British Prime Minister Winston Churchill and U.S. President Franklin Delano Roosevelt to ensure aid for Britain and its allies when this was critically needed in the early years of the War. The largest of these bases was Pepperrell Air Force Base in St. John's, with which media people in the capital were most familiar, but we knew very little about what they did at the more distant sites.

Harmon AFB

Thus, when an approach from the Press Club was made, the authorities at Harmon responded warmly and issued an invitation for media to be their guests for a tour of their base facilities. They even provided a military aircraft to fly us out there from St. John's, and back again later the same day. That was an offer we could not refuse. Media invitees who, like me, took the trip learned much about base operations, enjoyed the Americans' typically generous hospitality, and turned in a lot of good positive stories about how well those high flying jet planes were looking after our safety and security. Not until much later did we learn that, during takeoff for our return flight, our aircraft had a near miss with another aircraft, giving our hosts some anxious moments about which, fortunately, we were blissfully unaware.

Knob Lake

Which was just as well, for otherwise we might not have been quite so enthusiastic about another invitation, extended to us not long afterward, to take a much longer aerial journey into the wilds of

Labrador. This time, the offer came from the Iron Ore Company of Canada which was then in the throes of developing its huge iron ore mining operations in the Knob Lake-Schefferville area on the border between Labrador and Quebec. The company had just begun mining in that area four years earlier, and employed hundreds of Newfoundlanders. Interest expressed by the Press Club in visiting Knob Lake prompted negotiations with company PR people, helped along by a friendly Liberal member of the House of Assembly, Max Button. The result was a three-day tour in October 1958, with a party of about 20 news folk from St. John's boarding a luxurious company plane for the four hour flight to Schefferville. Iron Ore Company PR officials hosted the event along with Max Button and another memorable individual. Unofficial master of ceremonies for the entire tour was Greg O'Grady, whose flamboyant personality kept everyone in high spirits while media representatives were led around the Iron Ore company's vast mining operations.

The long flight northwards was a unique experience, simply because it seemed the fully stocked free bar was open almost all the way. For those of us normally having to count our pennies before venturing beyond a first beer, the temptation to take advantage of this unaccustomed largesse was irresistible. As a result, when we finally coasted in to land at Schefferville, we were floating on a silver cloud of mingled joy and stupor. So what was there to greet us as we stumbled out on to the ramp but - would you believe? - a friendly liquid reception! One jest of Greg's probably summed those first impressions aptly enough. That prominent "IOCC" company logo that we saw everywhere - he said, really meant "ten CCs" (referring to the popular Canadian Club rye whiskey).

Looking back on the serious highlights of the tour conjures up a myriad of vivid though fleeting images: everyone getting decked out with protective hard hats to withstand showers of mining dust particles; watching from a tour bus window a line of Montagnais Indians toting stacks of firewood on their backs; admiring the staccato showers of sparks kicked up by welding crews at work inside the long works buildings; struggling to keep up with facts and figures assiduously fed to us by project leaders.

An interesting side trip was the long haul between Schefferville and its Gulf of St. Lawrence shipping port, Sept Ilês, aboard the Quebec, North Shore and Labrador Railway. We took a fancy to its shorthand moniker, the Q-N-S and L. Called "Seven Islands" by Newfoundlanders,

Sept Ilês was a little more comfortable a place to live in, by all appearances. We couldn't help wondering how much of this operation was of benefit to Newfoundland, with so much activity on the Quebec side of the border. Later development was to phase out the Knob Lake-Schefferville operations by the early 1980s. However, mining began in 1962 at Carol Lake, Labrador, where the community of Labrador City has since became the dominant centre of the company's operations.

Just how well the trip succeeded in indoctrinating the St. John's media corps on Iron Ore Company mining, I'm not sure, but it did demonstrate the value of bringing newsmen to the scene, and the Press Club's ability to make that happen.

SPRINGHILL FUNDING DRIVE

One of the Press Club's most successful ventures got underway that fall with the launching of what we called the Springhill Children's Christmas Fund for the victims of a tragic mining disaster at Springhill, N.S. 178 coal miners were trapped deep underground Oct. 23, 1958, when a massive "bump" similar to a small earthquake, shattered the No. 2 colliery of the Cumberland mines near Springhill. It happened at the 14,000 ft. level - 3,900 metres below the surface. Rescue operations and the anxious vigil of miners' families were broadcast live from the site, evoking a tremendous wave of public sympathy across Canada and aboard. Initial success was made with the rescue of 91 miners, but little hope was held for the remainder. Dramatically, six days later, the sound of voices was heard by rescuers, and 12 other survivors were pulled to safety in what came to called the miracle of Springhill.

Moved by the tragedy befalling the 75 miners who did not return, Press Club members initiated a unique fund raising drive, based on the sale of copies of a hauntingly distinctive drawing entitled "The Miracle of Springhill". A starkly moving portrait of trapped miners huddling together underground waiting and hoping for rescue, it was drawn by artist Bill Werthman, then cartoonist with the St. John's Evening Telegram, and an active member of the Nfld. Press Club. Ten thousand copies of the drawing were printed and offered for sale, with all proceeds going toward the funding drive. The cards were printed by Bowden and Company which deducted from the printing cost a $25 donation toward the cause.

Memorial University President Raymond Gushue

THE MIRACLE OF SPRINGHILL N.S.

OCT. 30th, 1958   NOV. 1st, 1958

Press Club 03

agreed on a plan to have university students undertake to handle sales and distribution, while club members provided maximum publicity and advertising to promote the sales. On completion, the drive netted the remarkable total of $3,805.31 which was forwarded to Mayor Gilroy of Springhill for distribution to victims' families.

From Libel to Royals

Events of other kinds, both professional and social, kept club members of the Newfoundland Press Club very busy, well informed and quite well entertained as club programs hit their stride over the next two or three years. Regular meetings dealt with organizing the various special events on the program, but also found time for an occasional guest speaker. One of them was popular criminal lawyer James D. "Jimmy" Higgins who shed considerable enlightenment on the much discussed but little known laws of libel and slander.

On October 31st club members, spouses and friends staged a highly successful Hallowe'en Masquerade Dance at the Old Colony Club. It was one of the few times in my life when I ventured out in any kind of costume, so my choice of an unimaginative cowboy outfit was not destined to win any prizes. I did, however, get a souvenir cartoon to help commemorate the occasion! Our friend Lillian Macdonald, wife of Canadian Press correspondent Ian, showed up in a real "sack" dress, made from a flour sack in what seemed appropriately comfortable, considering that she was expecting delivery of her baby within a day or two.

Next morning, making his routine news check for the Telegram with police on overnight happenings, Tony Thomas learned that they had picked up on an impaired driving charge "a pigmy in a hula hula skirt." No direct connection was suggested with our Masquerade event, but one had to wonder!

Ahh, the Old Colony Club! That was the place to go for so many years in the 50s and 60s. A wonderful big dance floor and a lively and listenable band - the Prince's orchestra, or Chrissie Andrews, or Leo Michaels - and everybody danced in those romantic times. Over-imbibing was rare, as drinks were kept to sociable levels - the ladies sipping decorously on a Tom Collins or a Whiskey Sour, and the men savouring an India Pale Ale or a CC and Ginger. And at $5 double for a Hallowe'en event, the prices were not too bad either.

Social gatherings for Press Club members had a variety of venues on offer during that period - some taking place at the Ottawa Federal

Civil Service Club, where we met regularly, but also at a number of military bases in the area. Pepperrell Air Force Base at Quidi Vidi Lake was opened to us on occasion thanks to the kindly cooperation of its civilian Public Relations Director, Leo Shea. A St. John's man himself, he knew everybody and through his energetic example did much to ensure close and friendly relations between the American military and the people of St. John's. The fact that drinks were so cheap at the base bar didn't do any harm either to the willingness of the Press Club crowd to accept his frequent invitations to drop by for a social evening. Canadian forces PR people were also ever ready and willing to entertain the city media. One popular rendezvous site was at the RCAF station at Torbay (now St. John's) airport. Dancing, however, was a much better draw for spouses and friends of club members, so a number of these were organized throughout the year. One that many of us greatly enjoyed was held about the end of January 1959 at the Crystal Palace club in the Goulds.

The year 1959 was an exceptionally busy and at times traumatic period for all news media and indeed for all of Newfoundland. Fittingly enough, perhaps, in view of later developments, our first guest speaker of the year on January 15th was RCMP Superintendent E.H. Stevenson, discussing relations between press and police. He also outlined press corps procedures for the pending Royal Visit in June.

MUN President Dr. Ray Gushue accepts Miracle of Springhill poster.
Press Club 06

Another fund-raising experience for members came in March when the Press Club was called upon to give support to the Easter Seal Campaign for Crippled Children. At the request of the Sunshine Camp Association, the club arranged a dinner at the Old Colony Club with Whipper Billy Watson, the well-known wrestler and booster of the Easter Seal Campaign, as guest speaker. Our various media gave the event maximum publicity, and it proved a valuable contribution to the success of the campaign that year.

Working closely with US Air Force public relations people at Pepperrell Air Force Base, the Newfoundland Press Club played host at a mammoth reception for a huge number of national and international news media converging on St. John's for the June 18, 1959, visit of Queen Elizabeth and Prince Phillip. It was a totally informal affair, enlivened by the copious supply of inexpensive drinks as media visitors mingled with the local news fraternity. A highly successful and enjoyable event for all concerned, the evening came as a welcome respite from the din of political and labour troubles we had all experienced.

ANNUAL DINNER 1959

That fall's highlight event for the Nfld. Press Club was the October 14 annual dinner to which we invited Premier Joey Smallwood as guest speaker. Given the turbulent political atmosphere throughout that year, the very idea of inviting the Premier was not without some debate. Cooler heads prevailed, recognizing that he was owed the honour for two reasons - his position as Premier and his earlier years in journalism. Held at the Newfoundland Hotel, the dinner drew a good attendance from club members and politicians, including St. John's Mayor H.G.R. Mews and several cabinet ministers.

I took the opportunity to outline the objectives of the Press Club, with "the primary aim to draw more closely together the many diverse elements, organizations and personalities which play a part in keeping the public informed, enlightened and entertained." I noted the many activities the club had undertaken in the past year, including press tours to Knob Lake and Stephenville, fund raising for Easter Seals and victims of the Springhill mining disaster, and information sessions on the woods labour dispute.

Premier Smallwood devoted his remarks to a review of the history of journalism in Newfoundland, recalling some of his own experiences in the field. He mentioned handling his first assignment as a reporter by covering Armistice Day celebrations on horseback. Two weeks later, at the club's annual meeting, three officers - myself as President, Tony Thomas as Secretary and Charlie Bursey as Treasurer were re-elected, and Bren Walsh of the CBC was elected as Vice-President, replacing Pat Lees, who was leaving to return to England. The election took place at the Canadian Legion Club where agreement had been made for all upcoming club meetings and socials to be held. Legion representatives welcomed our business, and we liked the facilities and the low bar prices.

Another successful event followed November 19th with what was billed as a fur fashion show, complete with floor show! The gimmick was that the models were feminine only in attire, with Madame Edgar Squires, Mamselle Charlette Bursey and Senorita Belle Squires emerging as the stars of the show. Organizer Bill Squires got the entire local fur trade up in arms by calmly announcing that 'Continental Furriers of Montreal' were staffing the fashion show. The fact that no such firm existed was supposed to be kept a deep dark secret, even from the executive, until the merchants made with the war cries. We smoothed things over by agreeing to show some of their furs, so everybody was happy after all.

Money to keep the Press Club going was a constant preoccupation, but seldom did we have the good fortune to receive a cash donation. An exception of special note came one day in a most unexpected locale, the Premier's Office. Well, not exactly in the Premier's office, but just outside the door. There we were, three or four reporters, patiently waiting for the OK to go inside to hear an announcement Mr. Smallwood was about to make on some grave matter of state. What the subject was, we hadn't been told. Then the outer door opened to reveal the arrival of another participant in the pending announcement, the portly, commanding presence of one John C. Doyle, President of Canadian Javelin Ltd. Smiling amiably, he greeted us warmly and got us into conversation about our reportorial interests and concerns. One of us mentioned the activities of the Press Club which were then in full flight. "Oh," says John, "that's very interesting. I suppose you have to raise money to pay for those kind of things". "Indeed, I confirmed. "Well, then," he says, reaching into an inside pocket for a handsome billfold. "Here's something to help you along," and calmly slips me a $100 bill. We somehow got through the press announcement before, once safely outside, whooping and clapping each other on the back for getting the Press Club's first instalment toward that fine new clubroom we all had ambitions to open some day.

Social and business gatherings, except those held informally at the Legion, were fewer in number in 1960. Members did attend separate presentation socials and buffet dinners at Pepperell Air Force Base, and a Chinese dinner held at the Mousecellar, a recreation room at the home of club member Edgar Squires. A very successful pre-Christmas party at the Canadian Legion in December capped off the season.

ANNUAL DINNER 1961

The club's next annual dinner was held February 13, 1961, at the popular Old Mill Night Club. Again, Premier Smallwood was the guest speaker, and nearly 100 people attended, including many cabinet ministers, several prominent guests and a good representation of news men and women. An orchestra was on hand for dancing pleasure after the dinner.

In good form as usual, and steering clear of things controversial, the Premier recounted a few stories from his experiences before getting into politics. He recalled that, during the war, the city council of St. John's had refused permission for the Governor of Newfoundland to keep pigs in Government House grounds. When he and his family were living on LeMarchant Road, Smallwood wanted to keep goats on his property. He wrote a letter to the council stating that, if Mahatma Ghandi of India was allowed to bring goats to the Savoy Hotel in London, he saw no reason why he could not keep them in St. John's. "Perhaps to their surprise," he said,"the council gave me permission to keep goats on LeMarchant Road."

The Premier said the newspaper profession today was far different than when he was a young reporter, when newspapers took sides on everything, and reporters included their own opinions in their stories. Nowadays, he said, news reporting is much more objective. But he had a few suggestions. Newspapers and radio need a style book, he said, a standardization of phrases and writing styles. He said newsmen have a "frightful, vital and fateful" obligation to report only facts. A reporter should worship accuracy, he said, and radio announcers should strive for better pronunciation of Newfoundland place names.

Announcement was made at the dinner of the establishment of a $100 annual journalism award donated by E.J. Bonnell and Associates, and open only to members of the Newfoundland Press Club. Another donation which prompted due appreciation all around was a dinner wine serving contributed by Newfoundland Public Relations Ltd. A festive evening was had by all at what we considered an outstanding success.

So much for the good news. Unfortunately, thanks to a disastrously naïve gesture by the club executive, the event was a financial calamity. Our major flub: offering "no charge for drinks from 7:30 to 8:00 p.m." before the dinner. What happened, perhaps predictably, is that patrons took every advantage of such largesse - ordering doubles was in full vogue - and the close down order was late being enforced. As I reported to the club's annual meeting April 5, the drinks staggered everyone, and the Old Mill's total bill of $457 really staggered the executive. With other minor bills to cover, the $320 ticket sales revenue left the club a shortfall of $200.

Chastened by this setback, it was with mingled regret and relief that I turned over the problem to a new executive. In an election conducted by veteran Post Office public relations officer Bill Veitch. Tony Thomas, by now working with E.J. Bonnell Associates, succeeded me as President. Others elected were: Ed Quigley, Telegram, Vice-President; Charlie Bursey of Doyle Bulletin, Secretary; Edgar Squires, VOCM, Treasurer; Dick O'Neill, VOCM, Assistant Secretary; and Bill Croke, Telegram photographer, Social Chairman. The new team pledged to rebuild club finances and work toward attainment of members' fondest dream, our own clubroom.

However, after taking a financial hit on the dinner, a sensationalized Newfoundland Herald Story, reporting weeks later on the annual meeting, only rubbed salt in the wound. Headlines told the story:

STRANGE SITUATION

Premier Second Choice
At Press Club Dinner
Invited After Diefenbaker Declined Invitation

Perhaps not one Canadian would believe it, but it is a fact. Premier Smallwood was asked to act as a substitute for Prime Minister Diefenbaker at a dinner recently.

Did Not Know
It's a safe bet that Mr. Smallwood was also ignorant of this fact, when he accepted that invitation to address the annual dinner of the Newfoundland Press Club, held at the Old Mill Night Club.

Annual Meeting
The fact was disclosed at the annual meeting and election of officers of the Press Club held in St. John's a few days (ago.) A young reporter, Bob Lockhart, asked the meeting why Premier Smallwood had been invited

by the Club's Executive without reference to the membership. He said there was someone on the mainland he wanted to invite.

Membership
Reporter Lockhart made a motion that in future, guests be approved by the Club's membership before they were invited to speak.

Support
His motion was supported by a group of reporters from the Evening Telegram who, through Miss Sylvia Wigh, also objected to Mr. Smallwood's invitation.

Substitute
Replying to criticism of his Executive, President Nix Wadden said that actually Mr. Smallwood was second choice. He said negotiations had been going on with Ottawa to invite Prime Minister Diefenbaker. But Mr. Diefenbaker could not come because he was spending a holiday in the South.

President Explains
Asked why Mr. Smallwood was then invited, Mr. Wadden said, first because he is Premier of the Province, and secondly because he was a good drawing card and his presence would result in the Club making a few dollars on the dinner.

Increased Job
And then came the pay off - the Treasurer's report revealed that the club actually lost $250 on the dinner in spite of a full house, and the bill from the Old Mill was handed to a new Executive to deal with.

Amendment
Incidentally, Mr. Lockhart's motion was defeated, and an Amendment that the matter of inviting guests be referred to the New Executive for discussion, was passed.

The facts in the Herald story were basically correct, though the mock-scandalized tone, adopted by a staffer often critical of Press Club activities, put a regrettably negative slant on the issue. I did acknowledge that the executive had tried to get the Prime Minister as speaker, as seemed desirable since we had had the Premier at the last annual dinner. We had indeed tried very hard, since as early as January 1960, to persuade Ottawa PCs to have John Diefenbaker come to address the club for the annual dinner, then planned to be held that fall. We stressed the fact that this would have given him a good non-partisan forum on which to try to mend fences with the province after all the Term 29 and IWA strike battles of 1959. A formal invitation to this effect was sent to the Prime Minister April 7, 1960. Both W.J. Browne and Jim McGrath supported the proposal, but as negotiations dragged on without yielding a firm response until late in the year, we gave it up as a bad job, and invited the Premier for the February date, and he readily agreed. Considering that several of us on the Press Club executive were committed Conservatives eager to restore a little political equilibrium to federal-provincial relations, it was so ironic to get pilloried by PC-supporting club members for issuing the Smallwood invitation. Just goes to prove the old adage that you can't please everyone all the time.

Under the new Executive, the Press Club managed in time to resolve the financial problems, and to develop new fund-raising opportunities. Use of Canadian Legion facilities continued for some time, until circumstances arose that made this undesirable. One regular club member who was frequently among those visiting the Legion was Bill Werthman. A German-Canadian, he loved music and would often take the opportunity to play the piano in the Legion club, playing everything from classics to folk music. For the longest time, this bothered no one, but there came a time when a number of Legion members started to grumble about "this fellow playing German music in the Canadian legion." Speaking to Legion management, we were assured that this came from only a small minority, but it was plain that they were uncomfortable with the situation. Bill was quite willing to give up the piano playing, but the club executive decided, after some discussion, that it was probably time to move to some other meeting place.

Meanwhile, club fund raising efforts began meeting with some success, and by 1964, discussions were underway on the possibility of taking over an air force club which had been vacant since closure of the RCAF base at Torbay Airport. By then, funds of $2,700 had been raised through membership fee increases, donations and bingo. However, the proposal was rejected because of anticipated high costs for maintenance of the building, and attempts were begun to find a more convenient location downtown. Bren Walsh was then serving as Chairman, supported by Tony Thomas, Dave Butler (Telegram) and Tom Kavanagh (CBC). A new team headed by John Nolan of CJON as Chairman took over at the annual meeting in the Newfoundland Hotel in February 1965.

When Ed Bonnell became President of the Press Club in 1966, the drive for clubrooms reached its climax with the acquisition of the old Newman liquor building at the corner of Water St. and Springdale St. The Executive making this bold move under Ed's direction included Walter Lawlor (CBC) as Vice President, Tom Kavanagh (CBC) as Secretary, and Tony Thomas as Treasurer, with John Nolan as Past President. Working diligently to put the building into shape with a lot of mopping and cleaning and painting, the team succeeded in launching what they called the Springdale St. Club. John Long was hired as a full-time bartender/steward. As Ed recalls, "What fabulous times we had, and what great stories we could tell!"

All went well for the next two years, as the club drew a steady volume of business. There was even a club newsletter printed to promote the flow of activities. Giving strong support to the cause were 20 or so members of the Press Wives Club who catered to press conferences and corporate cocktail parties, and actually turned a handy profit. Its executive included Anthea Bonnell, President; Brenda Doyle, Vice-President; Dot Fardy, Secretary; and Pat Quigley, later replaced by Sylvia Thomas, Treasurer. Ed Bonnell and his executive were re-elected in 1967 and 1968. In the following year, Ed resigned because he had taken on a management position as Managing Editor of the Daily News, and Charlie Bursey took over as President.

Good times for the club were unfortunately short lived. The Press Club next year elected a new executive headed by Andy Tarvin, an American PR guy who had briefly managed the Daily News in a period when it was undergoing a change of ownership. This group decided to open up the club to general membership in a bid to attract more business, but that did not work out. Funds were running low and, despite various initiatives to reverse the trend, the clubroom operation could not be continued. One valiant effort to stave off disaster was the presentation of a musical - Annie Get Your Gun - at the Arts and Culture Centre. It did well, and was sold out, but a generous gesture in offering gifts to the performers more than ate up all the profits, because there were so many of them!

Even a sizeable loan from a club supporter could not stem the downward slide, and the Springdale St. quarters were reluctantly closed down. Very soon afterward, the Newfoundland Press Club as an entity also gave up the ghost. It had a good run, while it lasted.

BOOTS IN OUR BACKGROUNDS

Prior to the Premier's speech at the Press Club's 1961 Annual Dinner, he and I had a most interesting conversation - something I had not in the least expected. Although I had been in news reporting for several years, he and I had seldom spoken to each other before, except over the telephone. I was, indeed, rather uncomfortable because I had been very active in supporting political campaigns against him and his party, and I was sure he was aware of that. However, on this occasion, the talk was not of politics, but of boot making.

"Wadden", he said, "your family was greatly involved in the boot making business." "Yes", I said, "my great-grandfather had a very big business as a boot maker, and all of his five sons went into the trade as well." "Yes, I know," he said, "and so was my family."

I had indeed heard this before, but I listened with great interest as he told how his grandfather David Smallwood built up the same kind of business. In fact, both families had so much identification with the cobbling trade that some of their products got to be called by the family name.

My great-grandfather, Nicholas Wadden, was apprenticed to a shoemaker when he came out from Ireland in 1830 and founded his own business in 1843. His success as a boot maker was noted in a number of newspaper articles tracing St. John's history during the mid 1800s. Fred Jardine, writing in the Daily News in June 1935, recalled that the Water Street shoemaker shop of Nicholas Wadden was "quite a busy spot, sometimes employing as many as 10 shoemakers all through the summer." In addition to general repairs, "the chief business was the making of Wellingtons and soling and heeling skin boots. Sometimes as many as 300 pairs would be hanging from the loft at one time which found a ready sale just before ice hunting time." Writing in the Daily News July 23, 1935, P.K. Devine declared: "The name of Mr. Nicholas Wadden became a household word among fishermen of Newfoundland who used the word 'waddens' as a synonym for a pair of long boots."

Although taking a less active part in the business in his latter years, Nicholas earned the reputation of being, at 95, "the oldest man in business in the city", as he was described in a Trade Review report in 1910. "...he manages to reach his workshop nearly every day and put in some little time at actual manual labour. It is scarcely necessary to remind...readers that Mr. Wadden is a shoemaker because Wadden's boots are known all over the country...The old gentleman is still hale and hearty and may be seen any fine day taking a walk down Water St." He was then living with his son John at Springdale Terrace, 207 New Gower St., while another son, Joseph, carried on the business, later joined by his brother, Michael, my grandfather. Another son, Patrick, who ran his own shoe making business in the city, was the father of Fred J. Wadden, founder of the well known business firm of that name. The fifth brother, Nicholas, better known as Charlie, set up a shoe making firm in Montreal.

The Premier's grandfather, David Smallwood, who grew up in Prince Edward Island but moved to Newfoundland in 1861, set up a boot and shoe making shop in St. John's in the 1880s. In his memoirs "I Chose Canada," Joey Smallwood described some of the boots his grandfather made, and the promotional stunts he used to advertise them:

> He specialized in the manufacture of leather fishermen's boots. They were made mostly by hand and in three styles: one came well above the ankles, the other came up to the knees, and the third pretty well up to the thighs. It was then that my grandfather had a chance to show his real flair: he was undoubtedly the pioneer in advertising and commercial public relations in Newfoundland. He did everything in the book to make the name and fame of Smallwood's boots known to the entire population throughout the island....

He employed a Frenchman who called himself Count deCourcy (who wrote) verses...printed on cards and distributed in very large quantities. I remember one:

> Smallwood's Boots are the best of leather,
> Smallwood's boots they suit all weather,
> Smallwood's boots they are so grand,
> They are the best in Newfoundland....

> Over the front door of his shop on Water Street, David hung a huge boot made of planks strapped together with iron bands. Down the leg of the boot on each side were the words "Buy Your Boots At", and then along the length of the foot on either side "Smallwood's."...

My grandfather's greatest advertising stunt was performed in the Narrows, the entrance to St. John's harbour. The cliffs rise vertically from the water on both sides of the Narrows, and nearly every fisherman in Newfoundland used to pass between them by schooner at least twice every year. My grandfather...had a hole drilled horizontally into the face of the cliff, and into this hole he had installed a stout iron bar four or five inches in diameter and twelve or fifteen feet long. This was wedged tightly in place, and from it a huge boot was suspended by two stout chains. The boot was made of three-inch planks powerfully banded together with iron strapping. It was painted black on both sides and, in luminous paint - so that they could be read by day or night - were printed the same words as those on the boot hanging over the front door of his shop. That boot remained there for years and years. It was the first view of St. John's for everyone coming into the city and his last view as he left.

Joey's uncle, Fred Smallwood, carried on the boot and shoe business which he inherited from his father. Changing times, perhaps related to the introduction of rubber instead of leather in boot making, led to the gradual decline of the boot making business for both families. The cobbling tradition did not continue in later generations.

CANADIAN PRESS

Throughout my working days in the St. John's news media, I had a lot of dealings with the local representatives of the Canadian Press (CP) national news wire service. It was their job to report for national and international audiences on the major news events in Newfoundland, and they did so by assigning one reporter-editor to work in St. John's. Staff were assigned, usually on a two year basis, from a regional CP bureau in Halifax, and most of them were Maritimers. Their St. John's base was the Evening Telegram, but they routinely kept in touch with the other local media. As head of the news operations at VOCM, and earlier with Harvey's News Bulletin, I was one of the CP man's regular points of contact. The fact that we worked well together and got along very well forged bonds of friendship that continued well beyond our everyday working routines.

The first CP staffer, Joe McSween, came to St. John's about 1951, before I got into the media. His successor from 1953 to 1955 was Stewart (Stu) MacLeod, a Nova Scotian, who earned the respect of both government and community leaders as a highly competent reporter. His friendly and cooperative personality also won him many friends in the media community. He took an active part in Newfoundland Press Club activities and, although he was pretty much of a teetotaller, was usually the life of the party with his songs, stories and tinkling on his banjo.

He was rewarded for his journalistic competence during his St. John's tour when he scored the "scoop" of a lifetime. On April 24, 1954, he broke the sensational news that Premier Joey Smallwood's hand picked Director General of Economic Development, Dr. Alfred Valdmanis, had that day been arrested in New Brunswick. The arrest was made on charges of extracting large sums of money from industrial firms which Valdmanis had persuaded to set up in Newfoundland. Smallwood himself gave MacLeod the story, phoning him at home at 5 a.m., and it made headlines across Canada.

MacLeod eventually settled down as a senior writer and columnist in Ottawa for Canadian Press and later for Thomson News Service. We renewed acquaintance at the National Press Club, where he was among other things the prime organizer of the National Press Club Jazz Band. Stu also did me a big favour in that period by counselling my son Ron on his journalistic career, recommending that he start off at the Kingston Whig Standard rather than with an Ottawa paper. Ron did well in an eight-year stay at Kingston, and is now night editor of the National Post, Toronto.

Another Nova Scotian, Gerry Freeman, who took over the CP job in 1955 after Stu's departure, became a good friend of mine during his term in St. John's. His sometimes bizarre sense of humour fitted in well with the lifestyles many of us news types indulged in while we laboured at covering the news dominated by the machinations and melodrama of the Smallwood regime.

Following his Newfoundland assignment, Gerry did CP service in Montreal where he began off-hour studies in law, emerging eventually with a law degree with which he settled into a comfortable new career back in his hometown, Liverpool, N.S.

Our next CP staffer, Ian Macdonald, also became a close friend and companion during his 1957-59 stint in St. John's. He probably had the heaviest workload of them all during the tumultuous period of the bitter IWA loggers strike and political wrangling over Term 29 in 1959. He and his wife Lillian were frequent companions of my wife Madeline and me at social gatherings of which there were many during that heyday of the Newfoundland Press Club. On his departure for a Toronto posting that fall, he was succeeded by Joe Dupuis, a keen and hard working journalist who later went on to become CP Business Editor. In a letter written to Ian Macdonald soon after Joe's arrival, I expressed a little wonder at the hard pace he was setting himself. "Joe Dupuis," I said, "is burning up the wire with copy, and everyone is wondering how long it will last. He's really on the move, dashing in and out once or twice a day at the stations and two papers, and pouring out copy like an assembly line. I think everyone finds him a nice guy."

Jack Picketts followed Joe Dupuis as Newfoundland's CP correspondent in 1962, but although he participated in Press Club and other media activities, I did not build any close personal relationship with him or his successor, Dave Butler (no kin to the onetime Daily News photographer of the same name).

This was not surprising, since I was no longer the head of a news organization with whom the CP staffer normally deals, so our contacts were merely casual and social. That was part of the price I paid for changing jobs as I did - though the fact that I was now making more money and carrying less responsibility provided its own consolation. By coincidence, Dave Butler of CP and I left St. John's about the same time early in 1966, and we shared honours as special guests of a Newfoundland Press Club send off shortly before our departure. He quit CP and returned to St. John's a few years later to work for the Telegram.

Dealing as closely as I did with Canadian Press, I entertained at various times an interest in going to work for the wire service. At one point I approached Jack Brayley, CP's supervisor of Atlantic coast operations at Halifax, but found there were no openings. One of the few Newfoundlanders I knew who worked for CP around that time was my friend Cy Fox, who spent some time in Montreal and later in London. But a CP life was not for me.

CBC NEWS

When I first started in the news game in the early 50's, I would have liked to work in newspapers, but apart from night-time proofreading, an obnoxious calling in itself, I found no openings, so I pursued opportunities in radio. Landing eventually at Harvey's News, doing news for radio, I got to like it, and didn't think too much about moving elsewhere. But I did look around to see how the other guys did their jobs, and what I could learn from them.

One place I went to early was CBC because - well, because it was CBC. First I checked out the Gerald S. Doyle News Bulletin, because that was the granddaddy of all radio news - the most popular program on radio, at least for a lot of people around the province. Jim Quigley, who ran it in those days, was a first rate newsman, clever, highly knowledgeable, a good writer, and an all round good guy. He got into news after dropping out of a seminary, and probably before that he took a commercial class which taught him typing and shorthand. I often envied him these supposedly pedestrian talents, because nothing in my opinion can make news reporting easier and more efficient than the ability to take fast accurate notes, and to type them just as fast, and always legibly. I had to work out my own peculiar kind of shorthand, and learned how to type, badly, on my own, without ever rising to the ultimate of touch typing.

Like Harvey's News bulletin that I worked on, the Doyle News was produced well away from broadcast studios. It was done in the Water Street offices of Gerald S. Doyle Limited. A living legend for many decades, the Doyle Bulletin stood resolutely independent until changing times forced its demise in 1966.

CBC News, however, was a different kettle of fish, one might say. Cordial and welcoming whenever I dropped by for a chat, the news editor in charge, Melvin Rowe, was one of two senior staff who got into news from a unique background. Both were former telegraphers whose skills in that now obsolete craft were deemed appropriate qualification for broadcasting news on radio air waves. In time they added staffers of a more literary stripe, so the news product resulting was more than adequate to fill in the breaks between scheduled programs. One of them, John Puddester, was a former classmate at Memorial who delighted students with his wit and whimsy. Another was Darce Fardy, brother of a school classmate of mine, and destined to reach the higher echelons of CBC news administration.

Bren Walsh, whose career spanned several decades in news reporting and editing, became a senior CBC news editor after serving as news director at CJON and editor of the short-lived Newfoundland Weekly. A prolific writer, he worked as a political and legislative reporter for CBC, and was also an active correspondent for, and contributor to, various national media including Weekend Magazine and the Globe and Mail. After retirement, Bren authored a book, "More Than a Poor Majority", a critical examination of the British and Canadian governments' role in bringing about Newfoundland's entry into Confederation. His conclusion that the union was the result of a "plot to manoeuver Newfoundland into Confederation" was reached despite being frustrated by what he termed "glaring gaps in archival records."

Many who worked at CBC over the years had close connections with the news community. They included public affairs producers, such as Doug Brophy, Derm Breen and Dave Gunn; also photographers, such as Frank Kennedy and John O'Brien, both of whom converted into TV cameramen after years of newspaper photography at the Daily News. All were high quality performers.

Since salary scales at the corporation were generally higher than in private companies, thoughts of snagging a job in its employ did come to mind, but were not seriously pressed at the time. The operation looked much too staid and static anyway. Years passed, and situations changed when the CBC was granted a TV station licence in St. John's, and began hiring staff in the fall of 1964. CJON, in which I had then laboured for nearly five years, had won its TV licence in 1955, thanks to strenuous lobbying of the federal Liberals by Geoff Stirling and Don Jamieson. When staffing of the new station began, most of the news men and women in St John's, myself included, aspired to positions opening there. I did not approach them at first, but learned that three people from CJON, including two of my fellow news editors, Jack Howlett and Bill Bown, had been hired. Jack had worked with me at Harvey's News and VOCM. By the time I did enquire, I was told that all the jobs were filled. C'est la vie.

A kind of consolation: my niece Marie Wadden has been a senior CBC news and public affairs writer and producer for many years. I like to think my background in broadcast news had a little to do with her choosing this beguiling profession.

DAILY NEWS

Having gotten my start in the news game at the Daily News, albeit as a humble proofreader, I took a passing interest in its progress over the years, and was sad to see its ultimate demise. When I worked there, it was published by Robinson and Company, owned by the family of Hon. John S. Currie and run for many years by his son, Chancey, but all of this changed in the mid-1960s. Thanks to my old friend, Ed Bonnell, his story of its struggle for survival in its latter years seems well worthy of inclusion here:

> Robinson & Co. was taken over in 1967 or early 1968 by a group headed mainly by Andrew Crosbie, and including other members of the Crosbie family, Lewis and Miller Ayre, and members of the Perlin family. They brought George Perlin back from Queen's University, where he was a political science professor, to be the Publisher. He hired me as Managing Editor (1968). He had some very progressive ideas, and in fact spear-headed the move to buy out Blackmore Printing in Grand Falls with its various weekly or semi-weekly newspapers like the Grand Falls Advertiser, Gander Beacon, Lewisporte Pilot, etc. and added some new ones - Conception Bay Compass, South Coast Gazette, Humber Log, Labrador Aurora, etc. - to form the Robinson-Blackmore Printing and Publishing media empire in Newfoundland.

> This resulted in a number of bold ventures like the move to offset production in a new plant on O'Leary Avenue. However, the Daily News balance sheet was showing losses and, in the spring of 1969, the directors decided they had to downsize and retrench. They asked me to become Publisher when George returned to his work at University, and I agreed.

> We put together a small but effective team in news, advertising, and circulation, and had an incredible adventure in publishing. We launched such initiatives as the first Sunday edition, the first "Special Edition," like for the walk on the moon, and the victory of JRS at the

1969 Liberal Leadership convention, and the first colour comics section to be printed in Newfoundland, including our own strip "The Fishers of Bay Cove," drawn by the creative genius Ted Mills (our Director of Advertising) and written by all of us from time to time! We also introduced our own weekend feature section called "Newscene", a weekly business paper called "Trade News", a youth section known as "The Message", and other exciting projects.

It was a time I will never forget, with the hard work, bright ideas, and camaraderie of Phil Currie (Managing Editor), Noel "Hooks" Vinnicombe, (News Editor), Paul Sparkes (Features Editor), Ted Mills (Advertising and design), Tom Murphy (Circulation), and a team of great production people. But it took its toll. The company directors (still basically a Crosbie-funded organization) decided the Daily News had to go in order to concentrate on the new job printing plant and the growing weekly newspaper market that George Perlin had envisioned.

Some of us had fallen in love with the old "News", and I pleaded with Andrew Crosbie to spin it off as a separate operation, and I would carry on with it. He agreed (bless his memory) and supported my bid to the banks to buy the paper. So for the next year or so, the records show that I was the President of the Daily News Limited and the Publisher of the paper.

During that time we launched a free mass-circulation weekly known as "The Free Press" which helped Daily News ad sales, and I purchased Larry Hudson's successful south coast paper, "The Burin Peninsula Post." It couldn't last. I didn't have any personal financial resources, and was carrying a load of bank debt; and while the papers were actually making money, it wasn't fast enough for the demands of debt and for my own health. Two years of working day and night, literally seven days a week, had burned me out.

> Happily, it was at that very time (late 1971) that Bill Callahan and Jim Thoms became interested in acquiring the Daily News. Both of them were finished with their careers in the Smallwood administration, and were seeking new business opportunities. Again, Andrew Crosbie brokered a deal which got me out from under the financial burdens, gave me some money (mostly because of the profitability of the Post and the Free Press which I owned outright) and allowed Bill and Jim to purchase the operation and implement their own fresh ideas and energetic approach. That's when the "News" finally went tabloid, and so it continued for another 12 or 13 years. I went back into the PR business, and the rest is history. But it was a romantic era...

Bill Callahan took over as Publisher with Jim Thoms as Editor in 1971 and, together, they ran the paper until diminishing revenues forced its closure in June, 1984.

Born in St. John's and educated there and in Corner Brook, Bill Callahan began a long and distinguished journalistic career in that city with the Western Star. In 1952 he moved to St. John's with CJON, serving mainly as a news editor and later as sports editor. In 1959, about the time I went to CJON, he returned to Corner Brook to begin a seven year stint as managing editor of the Western Star in Corner Brook. In 1966, he won election to the House of Assembly as Liberal Member for Port au Port, and served in the last Smallwood administration as Minister of Mines, Agriculture and Resources and Treasury Board President. He also served for a time as CJON Radio and TV News Director.

Getting back into the newspaper field he went on to establish a unique record as the only person to serve as managing editor of all three Newfoundland dailies in the 20th century. Here's how he describes the ups and downs of his experiences with the two St. John's newspapers:

> Following the general election of 1971, on learning that Andrew Crosbie had decided to shut down the struggling Daily News, I proposed to the late Jim Thoms that we approach the businessman-industrialist with a

proposition to...keep the paper going: we would operate it as if we owned it, and hopefully buy it out of the profits. Extensive negotiations ensued and an agreement emerged whereby I took over as Publisher and Managing Editor and Mr. Toms as Editor in Chief. The decision of Albert B. Perlin, dean of newspaper editors and columnists in Newfoundland and Labrador after half a century, to stay on was a major vote of confidence in the new management. Thus St. John's remained a two daily-newspaper community for nearly 15 additional years, the News continuing to provide strong news competition in the local/provincial marketplace, and coming close to profitability in several years. Losses were kept at a minimum, as evidenced by the fact that at the end total indebtedness was less than three-quarters of a million dollars with good receivables of approximately $250,000 plus capital assets.

I think we can safely claim that The Daily News was the news leader in the city and the province much of the time - if for no other reason than the fact that it was a morning publication, and thus had a head start on the day. The entry-point to journalism for literally dozens of men and women who would become noted in various print and broadcast media and communications in general, its pages were graced by the bylines - to mention a few - of Josephine Cheeseman, Larry Hudson, Jay Callanan, Fred Armstrong, Darlene Sorrey (Scott), Harry Stamp, Bob Moss, Sean Callahan, Bette Murphy, Randy Joyce, Bob Woolridge, Suzanne Clark (Woolridge), Rick Callahan, Gary Zatzman, Bernard Brown, Paul Sametz, Ted Warren, John Furlong, Pat Roche, Paul Bickford, Mary McKim, Anne Murphy, Gordon French, David Benson, Fred Whiteway and, for two or three years, today's acclaimed novelist Wayne Johnston. In a real sense, The News was the "incubator" for other media.

There were first-rate sports writers like "Dee" Murphy, Fred Jackson and John Browne, very professional news photographers Myrna and Jack

Kielley, and columnists Bob Nutbeem, Rex Murphy, Don Morris, Ron Pumphrey, Margaret Kearney, Mary Darcy, Ted Power, Wick Collins, Ray Simmons, expatriate Gwynne Dyer, Dorothy Wyatt and, after his retirement from politics, Joey Smallwood.

The News "broke" many important stories, adopted a hard-hitting editorial style, and became noted as a crusading publication. This brought serious repercussions in the course of the lengthy trawlermen's strike when an angry Premier Frank Moores ordered Public Works Minister Tom Farrell to cut off all government advertising to the newspaper, an action that almost certainly played a large part in its eventual demise. "It's because of those damn editorials you're running on the front page," Farrell said in explanation of the cut.

The final issue of the Daily News, after 90 years of publication, came out June 4, 1984, with the page 1 headline "Looks like this is GOODBYE!"

A copy of that final edition is among my souvenirs.

TELEGRAM

While my only period of employment with the Telegram was on that part-time sports beat in 1955, I had much to do with many of its staff in Press Club and other activities. Long time Editor Mike Harrington and I knew each other since we met as Memorial College students, though he was much older than me. He mentioned to me more than once the fact that he had links with the Wadden family in an earlier generation. Steve Herder was the Managing Editor and Publisher of the paper for decades, and earned everyone's respect for his insistence on quality news reporting and editing.

Maurice Finn, who rose from copy boy in 1956 to one of the senior editors before retiring in 1994, worked with a remarkable assortment of newspaper men and women who dominated the pages of the Telegram during those eventful decades. Serving as a reporter, news editor, telegraph editor, and in various other capacities, Maurice put in 10 or more years as Managing Editor and took over as Editorial Page Editor to succeed Michael Harrington. He fondly recalls some of the outstanding personalities encountered in his career:

> The Telegram has been blessed with talented columnists during its long history but none more popular than Harold Horwood in the early 50's and Ray Guy in the 60's and 70's. So popular were they, readers would be waiting outside the Telegram building for the press to roll to get their copies early. Their target was Joey Smallwood. Horwood's "Political Notebook" hammered the Smallwood administration on a regular basis and his exposés angered Smallwood to such a degree that he cancelled all government advertising in the Telegram. Management of the Telegram refused to blink and Smallwood finally relented and government advertising in the paper was eventually resumed. Horwood eventually left the newspaper scene and became a prolific writer. He authored 22 books before he passed away in 2006.
>
> Ray Guy's column had the same effect on Smallwood as did Horwood. It left the Premier fit to be tied, often referring to the newspaper as a nest of Tories. Guy's column has been described by some as the catalyst that

led to the eventual defeat of the Smallwood government in the 1972 election. Guy was also a reporter and feature writer. His feature, "No More Coming Round the Mountain" about the demise of the "Newfie Bullet," won the national newspaper award for best feature story in Canada in 1967. He has also had a long and distinguished career as a humourist through his columns, his books, and his other work as a radio/tv commentator, actor and playwright.

Pat O'Reilly was the last of the old time journalists in Newfoundland. His career began with the Evening Telegram in 1919 when the only other reporter was a young Joey Smallwood. O'Reilly's beat was the police and the courts. Never without his trademark fedora and pipe, he relied on pencil and notebook as his only tools, and had no use for a typewriter. He was well into his 80's when he retired in the mid 60's.

While The Telegram had women's editors, female news reporters were a rare breed in the 50's and early 60's. One of the first of the hard news reporters was Joan Forsey, daughter of Phil Forsey who was a minister in the early years of the Smallwood administration. Joan also worked on the desk as a news editor.

Sylvia Wigh was women's editor in the 50's and 60's, but was probably best known for her involvement in theatre circles as a producer and director. She was succeeded by Eleanor McKim whose daughter Mary also joined the Telegram as a reporter, later moving to TV with the CBC. Sheila Gushue joined the staff in August 1970 and remained on staff for several years as a reporter and women's page editor. She also worked in television, and was communications officer for MUN's School of Medicine.

Photographers for the Telegram were many over the years, probably the most notable being Eddie Ringman and Nelson Squires in the 50's, Bill Croke in the 60's, and Dick Green and Bill Sully in the 70' and 80's. Squires moved to TV with CJON, Green formed his own photography business and owned an antique store. Croke went on to a career with the Canadian Press in Toronto and was involved in covering the Tokyo Olympics.

Bill Croke had another claim, if not to fame then to gratitude from both Maurice and me, because he was photographer for our weddings.

Bill Callahan joined the Evening Telegram as Managing Editor in 1987 in response to an invitation from Publisher Steve Herder, who had held that post himself for many years, and had hired him for a similar post on the Western Star many years earlier. Telegram ownership had been sold by the Herder family to Thomson Newspapers in 1970. As Bill recalls, he readily accepted this offer, but was to find that ownership restraints would pose serious challenges along the way:

> As Publisher, Steve had certain goals for the Telegram, one of them (in compliance with a Thomson system-wide policy) to bring out a Sunday edition, which we did. We also beefed up the editorial staff, added a slew of new columnists, and set out generally to improve the appearance and content of the paper. Substantial upgrades took place, as well, on the equipment side, particularly in the area of computers and in the pressroom.

Serious illness led to Steve Herder's retirement in 1991, when Thomson's named as his successor a self styled trouble shooter, Robert Mackenzie, of the Niagara Falls Review, with whom a "rather prickly relationship" ensued. A year later, James Palmateer, also from the Niagara Falls Review, was named as new Managing Editor, with Callahan reassigned as Editor of the Editorial Page and Maurice Finn moved to become Executive Editor. Eventually appointed as new Publisher in 1993 was St. John's businessman Miller Ayre. Further restructuring by the Thomson organization in early 1994 resulted in enforced retirement for Callahan, Finn and another senior staffer, Lifestyles Editor Emily Dyckson. Bill, however, continued as a regular columnist for another year.

In recent years, Bill Callahan has applied his talents to the writing of books as diverse as a novel based on the death of insulin discoverer, Dr. Frederick Banting, and a portrait of J.R. Smallwood as "Journalist, Premier and Newfoundland Patriot."

Thomson's sold the Telegram to Conrad Black's Hollinger Inc. in 1996, and it became part of the CanWest newspaper chain in 2000, only to be taken over in 2002 by the Montreal based firm of GTC Transcontinental Inc.

7

A Fateful Year - 1959

A FATEFUL YEAR

Dawning of the year 1959 ushered in a period of vast turmoil for Newfoundland, beginning as it did with the infamous IWA strike, followed by the uproar over term 29, and capped by a bitter provincial election. For me personally, there were momentous changes also - I bought a new car in May, was married at the end of June, quit my VOCM job at the end of July, worked as PC party PR person during and after the August election, and jumped ship to CJON Radio/TV in November. How I had nerve enough to do all that, and how I got my beautiful bride to go along with it, I can hardly credit, but it helped to be young.

Given all the other goings on that year, it's maybe a wonder that Madeline and I managed to work in that wedding day, June 27, the most important day of our lives. Not that it was any sudden affair, coming as it did after a long engagement, but it was fairly hectic, taking place amid an atmosphere charged with the tensions of striking loggers and feuding politicians. Even a significant wedding prelude had political overtones, as the bridal shower took place in Jim McGrath's parents' home and was hosted by his mother and sister, Joan. No politicking marred the wedding celebration, and everyone had such a good time that we were loath to leave before it was over. An idyllic honeymoon in Bonne Bay (later to gain fame for its inclusion in Gros Morne National Park) ensured us of happy memories long after such vital public issues all but faded into the ether.

THE BIG SNOW SLIDE

Logging strikes and political rowing weren't the only big news events in the winter of 1959.

As luck would have it, I was not at work Feb. 16, the night when a savage blizzard blockaded the entire city, precipitating a disastrous snow slide at the Battery that snuffed out five lives. The tragedy sounded a grim reminder of the perils that intrude some times on the rugged coastline where so many build and strive to protect their humble homes.

The storm caught us - my fiancée Madeline and me and another couple, Canadian Press correspondent Ian Macdonald and his wife Lillian - enjoying a little party in Mount Pearl with friends Bill and Margaret Werthman. What started as a gentle snowfall blew up into a massive blizzard, so we had no choice but to stay put for the night.

A wood stove kept us from freezing entirely, but it was a cool and uncomfortable night, especially for some whose footwear had been soaked in early attempts to get cars on the road. No spare beds being available, chairs and coffee table tops had to serve as makeshift supports to prop up our aching bodies. Discomfort gave way to hilarity at one point when a whiff of something burning was traced to Ian's shoes, carefully tucked in the oven to speed up the drying process.

Next morning, snow drifts were still at rooftop levels, and the best we could do was to wade hip deep through the drifts to nearby Samson's Supermarket to fetch bread and something else to eat. It was late afternoon before the rumble of snow plows encouraged us to set out for home. Even at that, the narrow track along Topsail Road was in zigzag pattern - at one point the zag took us between the gas pumps and the building at Parsons' garage as the highway drifts were too high for the plough to topple.

We were so relieved to get home at last.

Yet, despite a surfeit of aches and groans, and the stench of smouldering shoe leather, that night we spent by Werthman's woodstove is one none of us was likely to forget for many a day.

TURMOIL IN THE WOODS

A year of utter and sustained chaos began New Year's Day, 1959, with the ill-fated strike by the International Woodworkers of America loggers against the Anglo Newfoundland Development (AND) Company. Based in British Columbia, the IWA started organizing Newfoundland loggers in 1956 after being invited to do so by one of the existing local unions. They were seeking their first bargaining agreement since winning certification in the past year, and called the strike after the company rejected a settlement recommended by a conciliation board. As the year began, the news was dominated by the clamour of union loggers' antics and activities, especially when the company kept logging operations underway with non-union workers. Much was heard about the union's side of the dispute, but at first the company kept a low profile.

Stepping into this situation on behalf of news media, the Newfoundland Press Club invited the company to outline its position at a press conference. Accepting the challenge, company president Ross Moore travelled from his Grand Falls office to St. John's for what was billed as a question and answer session. Held Jan. 24th at the Newfoundland Hotel, the event served to put the dispute into some perspective. (AND later in the winter came up with a 32–page brochure, aptly entitled "Turmoil in the Woods", which outlined its position on the dispute.) Buoyed no doubt by its St. John's press conference success, the company promptly laid on a late January press tour to the heart of its logging operations in the Millertown area.

Victoria Lake

As VOCM representative, I was one of a dozen or so news media representatives to be invited on the tour. Our destination, Victoria Lake, lay deep in the central Newfoundland woodlands roughly near Red Indian Lake. We were flown to Gander and transferred there onto a ski-equipped Twin Otter for the ferry run into the deep bush. My most vivid memory of that flight was the scaringly steep dive with which the aircraft plummeted down for a landing on Victoria Lake ice. Everyone survived safe and sound - guess that's the way those Otters are supposed to land.

Fellow news and broadcast folk going along on the tour included Jack Howlett of CJON and reporter Don Morris and photographer Pat Dillon of the Telegram.

On the ground we were treated to a snowmobile ride - a first such experience for most of us - along winding logging roads until we reached the camp at the centre of logging operations. Inside, after a thorough briefing that emphasized the good life AND woodsmen enjoyed, we were invited to talk to the men clustered in their modest but comfortable living quarters. The guy I spoke to, in a moment dutifully captured by one of the photographers in our group, was a little shy, but affirmed that the working conditions were good and he was quite content with things as they were. I don't seem to have a record of his name.

A side trip out to the cutting area gave us a close up look at the way things used to be done, as we watched a team of horse-drawn catamarans piling aboard logs for transport to a truck loading area, en route to the Grand Falls pulp and paper mill. With briefings and interviews over, we climbed back into the snowmobile bound for another hair-raising flight aboard the Otter, and the rest of the journey home. Resulting stories helped to spread the company's side of the story, and gave all of us who went there a better, albeit one-sided, idea of what the furor was all about.

IWA Outlawed

Clashes between union loggers and strike breakers hired by the company caused serious unrest, but for six weeks no action was taken by the Smallwood government to resolve the dispute. Instead, in a memorable telecast Feb. 12, the Premier declared that the IWA strike was a failure and urged loggers to join a new government-sponsored union which he called the Newfoundland Brotherhood of Wood Workers.

To pick up on ensuing events, here are some excerpts of my VOCM reports on House of Assembly proceedings:

> Feb. 23: The House of Assembly lost no time today in plunging squarely into its most immediate problem, dealing with the IWA strike. The customary pageantry of House opening and reading of the Speech from the Throne being disposed of, Premier Smallwood took over the spotlight as he launched into introduction of a resolution condemning the IWA and calling upon loggers to withdraw from that organization to form a new provincial union. Specific steps to be undertaken by

the government in consequence of its intervention in the woods strike were indicated from three pieces of legislation, a notice of intention to introduce which was read during the afternoon session. These bills call for: amendment of the Labour Relations Act; a bill to prohibit general strikes, and a bill to prohibit secondary boycott...designed to prevent unions other than the IWA staging a boycott against paper companies.

The resolution proposed by the Premier received unanimous support from members on both sides of the House. The four Progressive Conservative members, led by Opposition Leader Malcom Hollett, rose in their seats, immediately following the Premier's address, to voice their support of the move to oust the IWA in order to safeguard the future of the pulp and paper industry in this province.

The stand taken by the Progressive Conservative opposition members, when they supported the Smallwood government's actions to end the woods strike, received the backing of the association executive at a special meeting early in March. Support, however, was not unanimous, as two members of the executive opposed a resolution which supported the Opposition members' action. I was one of them and the other was, I believe, Harvey Cole. I was really disgusted about this issue, and came close to pulling out of the executive altogether. Continuing the VOCM News report:

The IWA, (the Premier) said, asked themselves into Newfoundland; they were not invited...They muscled in here in the true tradition of gangsterism...in Jimmy Hoffa's tradition...Newfoundland has seen more lawlessness, more mob violence, more mob rule in the last 54 days than in all its history...Honest simple loggers had been turned into 'goon squads' by the IWA, befouling our Newfoundland life to the shock and horror of all our churches, without exception, all our press, and the overwhelming public sentiment.

The Premier also pointed out that of the 20-thousand workers who find employment in the woods with the

> two paper companies, 17-thousand are fishermen who gain marginal earnings, being only part-time loggers...I say to the House that the altogether wicked plan of the IWA is to confine logging to the three thousand or more full time loggers, to make them highly mechanized and supply AND and Bowaters with all the pulpwood they need. The IWA "would get a million of it in cash" and the 17-thousand fishermen would be left...with nothing but "fish and dole".

So wrought up was the whole province by the impact of the IWA strike that many were quick to pass judgment on who was right and who was wrong. Almost unanimously, news media editors and commentators supported the Premier's condemnation of the strikers and the harsh legislation he brought in to vanquish the union. But there were some dissenters. In Corner Brook, three top journalists with the Western Star - Ed Finn, Jr., Tom Buck and Tom Cahill, resigned in protest against that paper's editorial support for the government's move. The Western Star was owned by the Telegram at the time, so Managing Editor Steve Herder had to send out Telegram staffer Dick O'Neill to fill the gap left by their departure.

Harold Horwood quit the Telegram about the same time and for the same reason and he, along with Finn and Malcolm MacLaren, teamed up about a year later to publish "The Examiner," a pro-labour tabloid that was highly critical of the Smallwood government. It received initial funding from organized labour but, ironically enough, succumbed about a year later when its editorial attacks upon the Kennedy administration's ill-fated Bay of Pigs assault on Cuba angered labour circles in Canada and the United States. Still active at age 80 as senior editor with the Canadian Centre for Policy Alternatives, Ed Finn recently paid tribute to his Examiner partners Horwood and MacLaren for their lifetime dedication to "the struggle for a better world."

Certification Revoked

Continuing with VOCM news reports:

> March 4: Premier Smallwood today carried his legislative battle against the International Woodworkers of America a big step further as he sponsored a bill which, if passed, will revoke certification of the two IWA locals in Newfoundland and pave the way for his new

Brotherhood of Newfoundland Woodworkers to commence contract negotiations with the AND company. The bill prevents the IWA from making a new application for certification without the consent of the Lieutenant Governor in Council (that is, the Government) and forbids both the IWA and any other union or labour group from hindering paper company operations or attempting secondary boycotts. As Mr. Smallwood expressed it, the bill "doesn't put them (the IWA) out of Newfoundland (but) it draws their claws, and sends them west."

Government action is also proposed, the Premier revealed, which would in effect outlaw the huge Teamsters Union from Newfoundland. The Premier minced no words in his reference to the latter organization and its president, James Hoffa. Referring to a recent radio program in which Hoffa had unfolded plans as Mr. Smallwood termed it "to build an empire in Canada", the Premier raised his voice in loud protest: "The pimps, panderers, white slavers, murderers, man-slaughter-ers, embezzlers, extortioners," he charged, "are to take over in Canada."

Mr. Smallwood told the House he was ashamed to confess that it was not till recently that he learned that ..."Hoffa had already entered Newfoundland. The criminal", he said, already had established two branches of his union in Nfld., and already has a full time paid agent representing ..."the pimps, white slavers, dope pedlars." ...I'm referring," he said, "to Larry Daley*, Hoffa's man, who is not only a paid agent of the criminal Hoffa and his criminal union, but is also President of the Newfoundland Federation of Labour."

...And here the Premier disclosed wording of a clause which he said will be included in another bill to be put before the legislature shortly ..."Where any union existing in North America, a substantial portion of whose superior officials have been convicted in the courts of justice of such infamous crimes as white slavery, dope peddling, manslaughter, embezzlement or extortion, it will be abolished by law....We will wipe it out, blot it off the face of this good Newfoundland earth."

(* Larry Daley's wife, on hearing of this attack on her husband, reportedly suffered a nervous breakdown.)

Royal Assent

March 6: The two IWA locals in Newfoundland, one at Bishop's Falls and the other at Deer Lake, have been decertified by law, as of 5:30 this afternoon. At that time, His Honour the Lieutenant Governor, Honourable Campbell Macpherson, gave the royal assent to two bills, one of which specifically revokes certification of IWA locals 2-254 and 2-255. Legislation incorporated in these bills...prohibits the IWA, its officers and members, and representatives of any other union, from picketing the AND company or in an way interfering with that company's operations. It also prohibits secondary boycotting of that company's products. Fines for breaches of this legislation amount to five thousand dollars for trade unions, or 500 dollars for individuals.

... The two bills to which Royal Assent was given today by the Lieutenant Governor were altered considerably in detail, though not in important principles, from those first presented to the House...the Trade Unions (Emergency Provisions) Act 1959 ...dealt primarily with the revocation of certification of the two IWA locals as bargaining agents for loggers. The second... entitled An Act to Amend the Labour Relations Act...incorporated a number of new causes for revocation of union certification, as well as provision for banning of such unions as the Teamsters Union. ...Perhaps the most important change was the dropping of a phrase which would have empowered the government to revoke certification ...without assigning any reason for the revocation.

With the passage of this legislation, the IWA was defeated but remained defiant, backed by organized labour across the country as well as mainland news media, all of which condemned what was branded as the harshest anti-labour legislation in the nation's history. The situation came to a tragic climax at Badger on March 10 in a violent clash between policemen and loggers which left one policeman, Constable William Moss, dead. The police contingent included both RCMP and Newfoundland Constabulary officers assigned to the area.

In the wake of the riot, a call for RCMP reinforcements from the mainland was rejected by federal Justice Minister Davie Fulton, prompting the dramatic resignation of RCMP Commissioner Leonard Nicholson. The Diefenbaker government's clumsy handling of this situation was only to be outdone weeks later with the Prime Minister's announcement of its policy on implementing Term 29 of Newfoundland's terms of union with Canada.

Toronto Star Protest

While reporting from a distance on these dramatic events, my colleagues and I in the St. John's media, and more particularly in the Newfoundland Press Club, became personally and collectively involved because of the uproar caused by a single news report on the fatal Badger riot. As told by Richard Gwyn in "Smallwood: The Unlikely Revolutionary", the tragedy at Badger was witnessed by only one man, Toronto Star reporter Ray Timson. His account began:

> A column of sixty-six policemen waded into a throng of striking loggers, clubbed two of them unconscious, flattened dozens more while wives and children screamed for them to stop. Nine of the loggers were arrested. Most of them had been beaten to the ground, hand-cuffed, and dragged to their feet.

Timson's story was flatly denied by the RCMP and denounced by Smallwood. No inquiry into the incident was made at the time or later but, Gwyn stated, on the basis of all the available evidence, Timson's description was accurate.

Reading this account so many years later re-awakens a deeply uncomfortable feeling which assailed me at the time because of a hasty action taken by the Press Club concerning Timson's report. On learning of its contents, we in the St. John's media were almost unanimously sceptical about its veracity. A group of us got together in the press gallery of the House of Assembly (the old Colonial Building) for an extraordinary meeting of the Press Club to discuss it and to decide what if anything to do about it. What struck us most emphatically was that no other news organization had carried any similar report. The fact of the clash was reported but there had been no suggestion, other than as reported in the Star, that the police had taken the initiative and actually charged against the loggers. Given what we knew, or at least thought we knew, we were convinced that the Star report was erroneous, deliberately or otherwise, and we believed it should not go unchallenged.

We therefore proposed to send a message of protest to the Toronto Star. The majority of us - we probably had 15 or members present - favoured this action, but we had one or two bitter dissenters. The most vociferous opponent was Malcolm MacLaren, a Telegram reporter who was well known as a strong labour supporter. An Englishman who worked on the Daily Telegraph before coming to Newfoundland, he was not one of our more popular members - his argumentativeness was all too familiar to us already. (I once got so annoyed with him for this persistent trait that I stopped my car and told him to get out - I couldn't stand his antics any longer. Or maybe it was because he persistently called me "Nicky.") That sort of reaction doubtless affected our decision, as we voted by a large majority - with him strenuously opposed - to send off our protest telegram. I signed it as Press Club President.

In retrospect, and much as I hate to admit it, I'm afraid that Malcolm was right, and we should not have sent off that protest. The plain truth of it is that none of us at that meeting had any direct knowledge of what happened at Badger. None of the news organizations we worked for had any reporter on the scene, and we really had no basis in fact for our protest. It was all based purely and simply on our emotional reaction to the story and to its effects, as we perceived them, on the reputation of Newfoundland.

Not that the gesture had much impact, anyway. We did get an acknowledgement from the Toronto Star, and a few days later met with representatives of the paper - not Timson himself though. We ended up agreeing to disagree, and that's where it stayed. The protest incident does, however, indicate the depth of feeling engendered by the IWA dispute in that tumultuous year.

Maurice Finn, who encountered Timson at a newspaper gathering long after this incident, says Timson told him he had to be spirited away from Grand Falls the next day to catch the first flight available out of St. John's. The atmosphere prompted by his report, he said, was really scary.

TERM 29 TROUBLES

March 25, 1959, marked the ultimate low point for the Progressive Conservative party's efforts to gain any significant support in Newfoundland after a decade of rule by the Smallwood Liberal government. Already reeling from the turmoil of the IWA strike, the PCs gasped in bewilderment when Prime Minister Diefenbaker announced a "final and irrevocable" settlement of Term 29, the financial escape clause in the terms by which Newfoundland entered confederation in 1949. The term had provided for a review of the province's finances after eight years of confederation to determine how much additional financial aid would be needed to continue the levels and standards of public services reached in that period. A provincial commission which worked out its own calculations had recommended an additional $15 million a year, but the federal commission, headed by Justice J.B. McNair of New Brunswick and set up to do the required review, proposed an annual settlement of $8 million a year up to 1962, when a review was recommended, and thereafter.

In his memoirs, W. J. Browne described the announcement setting:

> After a brief review of the significance of Term 29, and the work of the McNair Commission and the Government's interpretation thereof, the Prime Minister stated:

> "It is proposed, therefore, to ask Parliament to authorize payments as recommended by the Royal Commission, but in our view the duration of the payments should be limited to five years, as both Newfoundland and Canada have recognized the difficulties involved in making projections from one selected year into the future, and it has further appeared to be quite inappropriate to provide for a fixed amount payable annually over a period of unlimited duration. A resolution will shortly be placed on the order paper asking leave to introduce a bill to carry into effect these provisions pertaining to the terms of union. The proposed payments will be unconditional and will be in final and irrevocable settlement of the provisions of article 29 and the contractual obligations of the union consummated in 1949."

Browne said he had learned that the Prime Minister was going to make his statement. "I tried to reach him by telephone but he was unavailable. I did get to speak to Don Fleming, our Minister of Finance, and I asked him to tell Mr. Diefenbaker not to make the statement he had planned, that it would do irreparable harm here. Mr. Fleming told me that unfortunately it was too late. The text of the message had already been distributed to the reporters."

In his comprehensive study "Smallwood, the Unlikely Revolutionary", Richard Gwyn stated that Diefenbaker had never read the statement before he delivered it in the House, and later ruefully admitted to a cabinet minister "I knew it was wrong the moment I said it." The statement, Gwyn wrote, was drafted by the Finance department and handed to Diefenbaker by Finance Minister Donald Fleming just before he spoke.

As Gwyn put it, "Diefenbaker was so out of touch with Newfoundland sentiment, and cared so little for it, that neither of the two Newfoundland Conservative M.P.s, Minister without Portfolio Bill Browne and Jim McGrath, was consulted about the date or even forewarned that the announcement would be made. Instead, they heard the news by chance over a car radio while on their way to a meeting outside St. John's."

I was plunk in the middle of this crisis since I was, not only reporting events as a reporter, but I was also an active executive member of the Progressive Conservative Party Association. Thus, next day (March 26) in St. John's, I was present at a special meeting of the Progressive Conservative Association called to discuss the Prime Minister's announcement. Bill Browne and Jim McGrath were there, also Senator John G. Higgins, and almost the full executive. Everyone was extremely upset by the announcement, and especially by the blunt and insensitive wording used. The meeting concluded with the despatch of a telegram addressed to the Prime Minister outlining the position of the PC Party of Newfoundland. The telegram stated that the terms of union contemplated no time limit on financial grants to Newfoundland under Term 29, and questioned the decision to "cut off" its provisions in 1962. The Prime Minister was asked to reply to this message by March 31.

Incredibly though in the circumstances not surprisingly, the telegram did not receive a written acknowledgment or reply. All that did happen was a phone call to association president Les Marshall from Finance Minister Fleming, speaking on behalf of the Prime Minister who he said was out of town. Browne remained in St. John's but, according to Gwyn, Jim McGrath flew to Ottawa to protest the decision in a meeting with Diefenbaker, but was met with an angry outburst against Smallwood.

In St. John's, Premier Smallwood lost no time in retaliating against the Diefenbaker decision, branding it as an "unspeakable betrayal of Newfoundland." He promptly ordered a three-day period of official mourning, dramatized by draping in black crepe the House of Assembly, the Court House and other government buildings. The Daily News appeared next morning with a banner headline "Newfoundland is Betrayed." Memorial University students paraded through St. John's bearing placards condemning "Diefenbaker: Thief and Faker".

Friction between St. John's and Ottawa simmered throughout the spring and early summer until reaching a climax in mid-July when Finance Minister Fleming introduced legislation giving effect to the Term 29 decision. Upon passage of the bill, Smallwood called for the House of Assembly to reconvene to set the stage for a provincial election, giving notice of a resolution which said in part:

> As the elected representatives of the people of Newfoundland, we will strive by all proper means to procure in the Parliament of Canada...the unequivocal acceptance of Term 29 as a solemn and abiding guarantee of the rights of Newfoundland, for which there can be no substitute. Our rights have been invaded by the Government of Canada, and we will not cease our resistance until these rights have been fully restored.

Before debate could begin, the dramatic announcement was made that two of the four PC members of the House, Jim Higgins and Gus Duffy, were resigning to form a new entity, the United Newfoundland Party. They were joined as new party members by two other PC executive members, John R. O'Dea and Harvey Cole. All four had been devastated by the Diefenbaker decision and had spoken strongly against it at the executive meeting in March. Their sentiments were shared by many but few others were prepared to quit the party outright, seeing little future for such a splinter group.

I attended a meeting of the Executive of the PC Association held that evening in the wake of these party defections. There were 16 members present. Business was brief but to the point. President Leslie Marshall read out letters of resignation from Harvey Cole and John O'Dea, and summarized the events leading to their resignations and those of Jim Higgins and Gus Duffy. To replace Harvey Cole as Secretary. I was named as Acting Secretary.

A motion to affirm support of the Term 29 decision of the Federal Government was put and passed by a vote of 15 - 0. W.S. "Bill" Perlin abstained from voting, advising that he preferred to defer a decision until later.

The President then read a draft of a proposed statement of policy. After some discussion, it was agreed that drafting of a series of statements be entrusted to a committee - W.R. Dawe, Mrs. G. Sparkes, Rex Renouf, L. Marshall and N. Wadden. In a news release issued the next day, the PC Executive "noted with regret" the resignations, and suggested:

> ...this action was the result of misguided patriotism on the part of these gentlemen who thus become unwitting instruments in the incessant battle waged in recent months by the Smallwood government against the federal government in Ottawa.

After such a dramatic birth, the United Newfoundland Party enjoyed a short-lived period of fame, but petered out within a couple of years. Higgins and O'Dea ended up joining the Liberal Party as cabinet ministers, but Harvey Cole rejoined the PC party.

In the House of Assembly, the resolution condemning the Term 29 settlement passed with only two dissenting votes by Opposition Leader Malcolm Hollett and his colleague Rex Renouf. Next day, the final House of Assembly session in the Colonial Building ended with Smallwood's announcement of his call for a provincial election August 20. The die was cast.

8

Progressive Conservative Party

NEWS AND POLITICS

Looking back on my activities throughout the 1950s and early 60s, I marvel at the extent to which I indulged my interest and involvement in politics while carrying on my work as a relatively objective newsman. True, I did not parade too blatantly in public my deep obsession with political activism and commentary. Nor did I try too hard to conceal it, especially from my employers and my co-workers. Indeed, the fact that I served on the executive of the Progressive Conservative party was noted in passing in media reports. Presence of a reporter on a list of party people didn't seem to bother anyone.

It was important, however, to steer a prudent course in coverage of political subjects, avoiding any hint of party bias in editing and reporting the news of the day. Fortunately, this sort of discipline came naturally enough so that, no matter how much the inner self seethed with frustration, news copy was routinely treated with reasonable fairness and restraint.

To be sure, zealots for one side or another of the political fence were not uncommon within the news fraternity, the majority rooted firmly in the Smallwood Liberal camp. Yet in general few overstepped the boundaries of objectivity, though leanings could well be surmised by the story choices, prominence and emotional thrust of coverage given. In an era dominated by the volubility, histrionics and volatility of its leadership, sober middle ground interpretation becomes an ever elusive objective.

PC PARTY DAYS

I was a confirmed opponent of Confederation and of the Smallwood Liberal government since its inception in 1949, so it was inevitable for me to take more than passing interest in political developments after returning to St. John's from university in 1952. I cast my first vote in the 1953 federal election but it was a few years before I got involved in political activity as such. The tremendous majorities won by the Liberals in both provincial and federal elections from 1949 to 1953 were too discouraging to prompt any such ambitions in that direction.

The provincial election on October 2nd 1956 brought on the first stirring of activism interest when neophytes Jim McGrath and Art Harnett put on a spirited and almost successful campaign in the then two-seat district of Harbour Main. Getting out to a few campaign meetings in the district was quite exciting, and sparked a growing ambition to get more actively involved in future.

That opportunity came in the federal campaign of the following year with the break through election victory of John Diefenbaker June 10, 1957. I was one of a group of eager young people, including my future wife, Madeline Roche, who volunteered to work on Jim McGrath's successful campaign in St. John's East. Stuffing envelopes was not an exhilarating task, but did make a worthwhile contribution to the electoral effort. Jim McGrath's campaign manager, Terry Trainor, was a dynamo in action, juggling telephones with expert ease as he kept on the heels of campaign workers while charming scores of supporters whom he let ramble on with the occasional "Yes, my darling," or "O yes, indeed, sir, that's a great idea". When the polls in St. John's East closed to reveal that our candidate had won, becoming at 25 the youngest MP ever elected up to that time, the lure of political involvement took hold for certain.

A further step in that direction came in January 1958 when Madeline and I casually dropped into a meeting of the Young PCs association, and promptly ended up on the executive. There was ample opportunity to get into active campaign work immediately when Prime Minister Diefenbaker called a federal election for March 31.

One of our first activities was to participate in welcoming celebrations for a visit to St. John's in February of the National President of the Young PCs, Douglas Jung. Arthur Harnett, Terry Trainor, (President Young PCs), Otto Byrne, Jim McGrath, Charlie Bursey and Leslie Marshall were on hand to greet Jung on his arrival.

A blue and white "Join with Jung" campaign ribbon remains among my souvenirs of that visit.

Someone in the Young PCs had the bright idea of inviting St. John's residents of Chinese origin to attend the party meeting at which Jung was guest speaker. This met with a gratifying response as a group of young representatives of the Chinese community turned out to meet him. They were an impressive group, ably demonstrating the extent to which, despite what had been for many of their parents humble beginnings, largely in food service and laundry occupations, they had advanced in prosperity and standing in the overall community.

Introducing Jung at a campaign rally, St. John's East M.P. Jim McGrath noted that the 34 year-old Vancouverite was the first Canadian of Chinese background to be elected to the House of Commons. Jung told the gathering that he owed his election to a new spirit "a new kind of Canadianism...free from racial and religious bigotry," and predicted a Conservative win with a comfortable majority. Following the 1958 election, he was sent to represent Canada at the United Nations. While taking his place, an usher told him the seat was reserved for the Canadian delegate. "I am the Canadian delegate," he said. A film biography of Jung under that title has recently been released.

Putting in many hours of volunteer work for the campaign, I helped out with publicity, had a hand in writing a number of campaign speeches, and even got into some fun projects in advertising. At one point I teamed up with my friend Bill Werthman in producing campaign posters boosting our candidates. Bill did the cartoons while I did the captions. One of my favourites: supporting Conservative challenger Ged Winter in Bonavista-Twillingate was the sonorous but over confident gibe "A Bitter Pill for Pickersgill." For Trinity-Conception, we offered the hangdog image of a crestfallen Liberal supporter muttering "I Didn't Vote for Harnett, Darn It." Unfortunately for Harnett, too many others did not vote for him either, as he lost by 3,700 votes to former St. John's city councillor Jim Tucker.

The Diefenbaker government scored a landslide victory, winning 208 out of 265 Commons seats, the greatest majority ever up to that time. Jim McGrath captured an overwhelming majority with 17,894 votes, almost doubling those for his Liberal opponent Greg O'Grady (well remembered by me for his life of the party role in our 1958 press club tour of Knob Lake.) In St. John's West, W.J. Browne drew 15,953 votes for a decisive win over Liberal candidate Dr. Leonard Miller who got 10,338 votes. The five other Newfoundland ridings all remained loyally Liberal though with reduced majorities. Closest fight was put up by PC candidate Tom Cahill, with 10,338 votes in Humber-St. George's, behind Liberal Herman Batten at 13,468 votes. A friend from Memorial University days, and earlier at St. Bon's, Tom was also a journalist at that time, and we sometimes corresponded on political matters. He later became one of Newfoundland's best regarded playwrights.

A fitting celebration of the double victory in St. John's ridings was held April 9th at the PC Victory Dance held at the Old Colony Club and organized by the Young PCs. A few speeches, cutting and sharing slices of a giant victory cake, and much rejoicing and exchanging of mutual congratulations marked that memorable evening. Thank you notes from Jim McGrath and W.J. Browne for campaign support are among my souvenirs from that landmark election.

A few weeks later, as W.J. resumed his position as Minister without Portfolio, I approached him on the possibility of serving as his Private Secretary. I did so by phone, and in a follow-up letter, after being told by Tom McNamara, who had been performing these duties, that he now wished to resign from that position. Browne's reply letter in early

PC Victory Dance celebrants: Madeline Wadden, Bill and Margaret Werthman, Craig and Eleanor Dobbin, Betty Lockhart, Bill Squires, Mary Hollett.

May indicated he had not yet decided upon this matter. When the decision was made, not long after, defeated candidate Art Harnett was appointed as his Executive Assistant. I thought it was worth the try anyway, and Art and I kept in fairly close contact throughout his term in that role.

My involvement in PC party activities stepped up to another level when I was elected to the Nfld PC Assn executive at the annual general meeting on June 25, 1958.

PC Association

Inner workings of the PC Association were run by the Policy Committee of which I as an executive officer became a member. It was in fact the group that ran the party, and dealt only marginally with policy matters.

I took on responsibility for publicity, but quickly became just as much involved in planning, program, organization and what there was of policy. It was obvious from the start that very little was in place in any of these areas, but there seemed to be a lot of willingness to make things happen. A hoped for goal was to organize a provincial party convention, preferably outside of St. John's. Another proposal was for the appointment of a provincial party organizer. (A start on organizing party branches outside the capital had been made a year or two earlier by hiring journalist Charlie Bursey as a federal party organizer, using funds from the national party, but he stepped down after one year.)

As one positive new step, development began on a series of 15-minute radio talks by the four Newfoundland M.H.A.s, using free air time reserved for that purpose. Also, I undertook to produce a newsletter to communicate with branches on party activities. In a discussion on how to get better media coverage, one member ventured the bold, but daft, notion to supply the Telegram with a weekly column to replace Harold Horwood's Political Notebook! Rex Renouf urged other M.H.A.s to organize district branches. He had started doing so in St. John's South but none of the others seemed interested.

As for party organization, work was needed to revise and update the association constitution to form the basis of a truly provincial organization instead of a St. John's group purporting to represent the whole province. One provision in the resulting document set the association membership fee at 50 cents per person. Moreover

For the purpose of maintaining the Headquarters of the Association, all subsidiary organizations shall contribute the sum of ten cents annually per person to this Association. This payment shall entitle the members of such subsidiary organization to membership in this Association.

There was some discussion of a proposal to drop the "ten cent" formula and instead to raise the membership fee to $3 to be distributed equally among the provincial, federal and the branch or district association.

Patronage

Sitting in for policy committee meetings was a telling experience for me as discussions were quite frank, expressing the basic concerns and interests of those around the table. Most if not all of the PC leaders had joined the party because they had fervently opposed Confederation and despised Smallwood and the Liberals for having brought it into being. Les Marshall, the President, had worked with one of the local clothing companies that was put out of business by confederation, and he remained particularly bitter for that reason. Bill Perlin, one of the wilier backroom strategists in the group, was a brother of Daily News editor and columnist Albert Perlin. Others included businessmen, lawyers, other professionals, and a few journalists.

I found myself rather shocked at the reaction of some of the executive when discussions about Prime Minister Diefenbaker touched on the prairie populist's moralistic approach to party patronage. It seems that Diefenbaker frowned mightily on the practice of rewarding one's friends and supporters with contracts and fiscal favours, so those expecting a brighter future from the new majority government were destined for disappointment. Having witnessed the excesses of patronage enjoyed by Liberal opponents under the Smallwood regime, faithful PCs were deeply incensed. Thus was spawned some of the deep distrust and disenchantment with the federal Tories that brought on before long - greatly accelerated by the IWA strike and term 29 debâcles of 1959 - a serious drop off in PC electoral support.

PC PR - FRONT MAN FOR DALTON CAMP

In what may have been the boldest gamble of my somewhat chequered working life, I left a relatively secure radio news job in midsummer 1959 to become a political PR man. Bold enough, considering that I had bought a new car and was married just months earlier. And here was I going to work for the Progressive Conservative party which Premier Joey Smallwood vowed to wipe out entirely in a snap election August 20.

Premier Smallwood called the election July 28 immediately after the House of Assembly passed a resolution condemning the Diefenbaker government's decisions on Term 29 of the terms of Confederation. Having handled publicity for the PC Association for some time, I was asked to do the same for the election campaign, and, perhaps in a weak moment, I agreed to do so.

I got a leave of absence from VOCM to take on this work which was at first expected to last only through the election campaign. After the election, I was asked to continue my services for what might be an indefinite period, and I again agreed. Funding for the job was provided by the National PC Association, which seemed a good thing at the time but, as I might have guessed, it was not to last for ever. A long way short of that, in fact, since the funds dried up and the gig was discontinued at the end of October. By that time, as it happened, neither I nor VOCM was keen about me returning into its fold, so I had to find another job.

My work during the campaign was focussed on publicity and advertising, churning out press releases, keeping media advised of candidates' movements and events, and preparing and placing campaign ads, mostly for individual candidates. The publicity activities were hectic and demanding, but no problem to deal with. However, I had to learn fast and lean on others for help on the advertising side, with which I had had little experience. In fact I had not touched advertising since my volunteer days as business manager of the Memorial University Muse in 1952-53.

My office was set up at PC headquarters in the Renouf Building on Church Hill, conveniently close to both the Evening Telegram and the Daily News, as well as VOCM and the CBC. Among those working at headquarters was Marguerite Reid, whom I knew pretty well as a journalist who covered mostly social events and wrote gossip columns about local celebrities. (Many years later I learned from Harold

Horwood's autobiography "Among the Lions" (Killick Press 2000), that she got into a long and intimate relationship with him in the mid 1950s. I never guessed!)

Working on that campaign was an eye-opener, especially when I learned that I would be working with a deliberately silent "partner." Sent in to inject professional expertise into the campaign was none other than Dalton Camp, the advertising and speech writing guru largely responsible, along with national director Alistair Grosart, for the successful 1957 federal campaign that brought John Diefenbaker to power. Jim McGrath had requested his services for what everyone knew was going to be a challenging uphill campaign. Camp, then in his prime at 37 with several provincial elections also under his belt, holed up in a suite at the Newfoundland Hotel, with strict orders for no one to divulge his location or even the fact that he was in town.

What he accomplished over that short three weeks was extraordinary, given the desperate circumstances the PC party found itself in as it began. The entire province was in uproar since February over the tumultuous IWA strike and a succession of disastrous blunders by Prime Minister Diefenbaker and his ministers on both the IWA and Term 29 issues. Only one week earlier, the provincial PC party had split asunder when, in protest against the Diefenbaker decisions, two of its four Members of the House of Assembly and two high ranking executive members resigned to form a new United Newfoundland Party. Premier Smallwood demanded that the Conservative party be wiped out.

Controlled Campaign

Dalton Camp took total control of campaign communications, orchestrating a series of masterful television talks by Opposition Leader Malcolm Hollett. Demonstrating an uncanny mastery of the issues and story lines most likely to influence voters, with a pithiness of phrase to rival Smallwood's command of campaign oratory, he personally wrote all of the speeches. Moreover, he coached, coaxed and inspired flawless delivery of the speeches from Hollett - an unbelievable feat given the Opposition Leader's usually uneven and rambling mode of presentation. Texts of TV addresses were rushed to other media, earning further coverage and favourable comment.

As election day neared, national media interest significantly increased, as did awareness of the remarkably improved quality of the PC party campaign. I had a nervous moment one day on getting a phone call from a mainland based reporter, then spending a few days in St. John's, who asked innocently if Dalton Camp was involved in our campaign. "No, not at all," I bold facedly replied. "Why do you ask?" He backed away, though sounding unconvinced. When I told Camp about it - he just laughed. He knew the reporter - I think his name was Hoyt - as they were both from New Brunswick - and warned me that this guy was pretty astute. The question came up again later, but with no confirmation forthcoming from us, and no Camp sighting at the Nfld. Hotel or elsewhere, no story of any mysterious backroom campaigner ever appeared.

Centrepiece of the Conservative campaign platform, also composed and marketed by Camp, was the Progressive Conservative Party's "Charter for a New Deal for Newfoundland". Principal features, apart from ambitious tax and spending proposals, were for repeal of the contentious labour legislation enacted five months earlier, and acceptance of the federal government's offer of special grants to Newfoundland under a review slated for 1962. Dubbed the Hollett charter, the document called for cuts in sales tax and "abolition of the yearly burden of school textbook costs" by providing free school books for grades one to eleven. A particular aim was to cut out the "vicious" sales tax on food. "No other province in Canada, although seven others have a sales tax - has a tax on food - it is wholly unfair and unnecessary". Savings to offset revenue losses due to these cuts were to be achieved "by cutting out reckless waste, corruption, greed and foolish ventures." Other proposals touched on negotiating for higher federal spending to complete the Trans Canada Highway in Newfoundland; also special funds for small loans to fishermen and to people wishing to build homes in rural and outport Newfoundland; a flying medical clinic service, and cost sharing on roads to resources and rural electrification.

PC candidates were entered in 32 of the 36 seats in the campaign. When the polls closed, both sides had something to cheer about. Liberals had performed another sweep, capturing 31 of 32 seats in which they put up candidates. The two PCs surviving in the pre-election House - Malcolm Hollett and Rex Renouf - were defeated. Running for his first and only time in St. John's West, Smallwood himself beat Hollett, while Rex Renouf was defeated by UNP candidate John R. O'Dea in St. John's South, which the Liberals did not contest. However, contrary to Smallwood's avowed objective - three other PC candidates were elected - Jim Greene in St. John's East, Dick Green on

Bell Island, and Albert Furey in Harbour Main. Greene's win was an uphill victory as he defeated UNP candidate J.D "Jimmy" Higgins, who had won the seat handily as a Conservative in 1949 and 1951. That seat too had no Liberal candidate. One other United Nfld Party member who ran unopposed by the Liberals, A.M. "Gus" Duffy, was elected in St. John's Centre.

In the number of votes cast, PCs won over 25% as compared to 57% for the Liberals, 8.5% for the United Newfoundland Party and 8% for the NDP, which campaigned strenuously in protest against the government's harsh labour legislation. Although far from ideal, the election outcome was in a small way a triumph for the PCs, thwarting the Premier's much trumpeted boast to wipe them out, and opening the door for a younger, fresher generation to reshape the party into a credible alternative to the Smallwood Liberals. Escaping annihilation while presenting a cohesive and positive program could not have been achieved, in my view, without the driving force of Dalton Camp's campaign management skills.

Toward the end of the campaign, I indulged in something I seldom have done by taking modest $5 bets on five districts. To my great satisfaction, I won them all - for example, by backing the three successful PCs and forecasting the demise of some UNP challengers. Just my luck, however - the guys I bet with never did come around to pay up.

Much higher stakes applied in a wager on the Conservative campaign that was taken with some high roller Liberal backers not long before election day. The magnitude of the bet was, if I recall correctly, $5,000 - a princely sum in that era. The placement of the wager fell to me to communicate to the other side - a service I undertook at the urgent behest of my thoroughly anonymous mentor, Dalton Camp. The purported source of the bet was not disclosed, and it took various exchanges of phone calls before opposite numbers began to treat it seriously. Negotiations for a time blew hot and cold but eventually petered out, and boy, was I relieved! As the only identifiable individual originating this gambling ploy, I was getting quite nervous that I would somehow be caught in the middle. Fortunately, enthusiasm waned, and no high stakes money changed hands. Just as well, too. Camp finally confided to me that there was no high stakes bettor. The whole thing was a playful hoax, conjured up by him to try to shake up Liberal arrogance. Don't know if it worked any such magic. It shook me up, though, while it lasted.

Post Election Activities

In the aftermath of the election, party members, including both successful and defeated candidates, looked back on the election campaign and undertook a review of what went right and what went wrong. Results of this review were presented at a two-day Candidates Meeting held in mid-September under the chairmanship of new house leader Jim Greene. 17 candidates attended. National PC Party director Alistair Grosart addressed the group, admitting that certain mistakes had been made at Ottawa but stressing the fact that the PC party had defeated Premier Smallwood's efforts to wipe it out, and it was now in a much stronger position than formerly. Reports by various candidates highlighted the need to improve access to federal government jobs and contracts for PC supporters and public awareness of PC party responsibility for new federal benefits and programs. They called for inclusion of candidates on the party executive and the appointment of a liaison officer to provide information and publicity support for the districts.

Working on PC party publicity following the hurly burly of the election was only in sporadic demand, so my tasks inevitably broadened to cover a variety of activities to support organizational development and future planning. I did provide support as needed to the new House of Assembly members, particularly Jim Greene who was chosen House leader within days of the election. A lengthy profile of the new leader is among souvenirs of that period. With no sign of an early opening of the new legislative session, duties were concentrated on maintaining contacts with PC Association groups and defeated candidates, and promoting public awareness of party activities.

That final month was generally a quiet time, coming as a welcome respite while I tried to determine my future prospects. Hearing at last that job funding would end October 31st proved the reality check I needed to plot a new career move.

It was Jim McGrath who solved my problem by having a word with Don Jamieson, recommending that I be hired as a CJON news editor. Jim had worked at CJON as advertising sales manager before winning his Parliamentary seat. Jamieson agreed, and in due course I bid goodbye to my brief flirtation with party politics to return to honest work in the broadcast news game.

PC Convention 1959

I went to two national conventions of the Progressive Conservative Association of Canada in Ottawa - in 1959 and 1964 - both of them in a dual capacity as a journalist and as a delegate. That was a mixed blessing, as I learned only too well at the latter event. But at least on both occasions I could say that I got my picture in the paper.

I didn't really expect to get to the first one. It was set for Nov. 30-Dec 2, 1959, and I had just gone to work at CJON Radio-TV on November 1st. Having worked as PC PR man in the three previous months, and been actively involved in the party all year, I was chosen as one of three Young PC delegates for the convention. The party would be paying my expenses. So I had to give it a try, and to my pleasant surprise, CJON management agreed to let me go, provided I would cover it for the station.

Being a new employee, I didn't want to trumpet my Party connections, and did my reports strictly from a news point of view, keeping a low profile on my actual convention participation. Well, I tried. The Toronto Globe and Mail, under a grammatically incorrect top of page headline "Excited Uproar Greets Choice of Young PCs' Chief", carried Dec. 2nd a full size photo of the winner surrounded by delegates, none more prominently full faced than yours truly. Thankfully I was not identified by name. The same photo showed up, even larger and clearer, in Saturday Night magazine's Dec. 19th edition, highlighting a feature story on the Tory convention. So much for that low profile!

That 1959 convention was a huge event, some 1,800 delegates from coast to coast, everyone flushed with the unaccustomed glow of celebration after the March 31, 1958, landslide election victory of the Diefenbaker government. The unprecedented majority of 208 out of 265 PC seats was seen as assurance of many happy returns for a party that had for so long languished in opposition. Not only that - Conservatives by that time were in power in five provinces - Ontario, Manitoba, Nova Scotia, New Brunswick and Prince Edward Island. Indeed, that Saturday Night article by Edwin Copps led off with the confident prediction that "The Tories are going to stay in power for a long, long time. The administration of Prime Minister John Diefenbaker (or his political heir, if need be) may very well beat the record 22-year run of their durable Liberal predecessors under Mackenzie King and Louis St. Laurent." Or maybe not!

This was my first time in Ottawa, and, on the day before sessions began, I had a helpful and fun-filled guide to show me around - Terry Trainor. Once my Scoutmaster, an athlete well known as a defenceman on the champion St. Bon's hockey team and campaign manager for Jim McGrath's election victories in 1957 and 1958, Terry was there as President of the Young PCs. We roomed together at a Rideau St. motel 10 minutes away from the convention site, the sumptuous Chateau Laurier. He took me on a tour of Parliament Hill - we got an exclusive walk around with a Hill staff guide on a frosty tourist-free morning. We wined and dined in the Chateau and drifted into hospitality suites to mingle with other delegates, including our third YPC rep from St. John's, Joan McGrath, Jim's younger sister. But he couldn't prevail on me to join him in satisfying his sudden whim to go for a Turkish bath. I took off instead to visit my cousin Patsy (O'Driscoll) McDougall whose husband Wally worked with the Fisheries Department.

The Newfoundland contingent at the convention were rather less ebullient than their mainland colleagues. The strains of Smallwood's shellacking in the August provincial election and the damage done by the disastrous Term 29 and IWA strike fumbling by the Diefenbaker regime were all too evident. A distinct coolness toward the Prime Minister marred for us the otherwise frolicsome atmosphere around us.

NEW HOUSE IN THE CLOUDS

After sinking to depths of discord amid the controversies of the troubled year of 1959, the political landscape of Newfoundland entered a promising new era in the spring of 1960. It was eight months to the day following a provincial election which changed the faces, if not the fortunes, of the Progressive Conservative opposition.

Lieutenant Governor Campbell Macpherson presided April 20, 1960, over the 32nd general assembly of the Newfoundland House of Assembly in its spanking new quarters in an upper floor of the 12-storey Confederation Building, newly built as the provincial government headquarters, and new home of the provincial legislature.

Flushed with his landslide victory in the August election, which returned 31 Liberals, three Progressive Conservatives and two from the fledgling United Newfoundland Party, Premier Smallwood was in celebratory mood, praising this "gracious and spacious" new chamber. Opposition Leader Jim Greene had a different take: "God bless our mortgaged home", he said, and confessed that he felt much like "Alice in Wonderland at the Mad Hatter's Tea Party."

The 31-year old lawyer succeeded to the Opposition Leader's position following the election. As a former Rhodes Scholar and talented speaker and debater, he was an obvious choice for the role. Contrasting sharply with his predecessor, Malcolm Hollett, he aggressively cultivated close ties with the federal PC organization, visiting Ottawa three times in his first eight months. In November, he led the Newfoundland delegation attending a three day national convention of the Progressive Conservative Association of Canada in Ottawa. He told the convention the Newfoundland government was the "toughest nut" for PCs in Canada to crack, but he was confident in his party's ability to put out of office "the last Liberal Government in Canada." Bold words, but fated to be forgotten when Tory prospects at the national level dimmed drastically within 12 months, and died in the following year. Prospects at the provincial level did not fare much better.

After surviving seven active but frustrating years in the Progressive Conservative Opposition facing the steam-roller might of Joey Smallwood's Liberal government, Malcolm Hollett escaped to a far more comfortable political career in October 1961 when he was appointed to the Canadian Senate. His appointment by Prime Minister John Diefenbaker came two years after the 1959 election when he was defeated by Smallwood in punishment for his defence of Diefenbaker's policies on Term 29. He had served as Progressive Conservative MHA for St. John's West since 1952, and as Opposition Leader since 1953.

A native of Burin, Hollett served with the Royal Nfld Regiment in the First World War, and won a Rhodes Scholarship for studies in mathematics at Oxford University. He served for 25 years as a Magistrate stationed at Burin, Bell Island and Grand Falls. I knew two of his four children, Mary, who worked with me at VOCM, and Harry, who was a fellow student at Memorial University.

STALEMATE IN ST. JOHN'S WEST

All the ferment and fireworks of the 1959 battles over Term 29 bubbled again to the surface when voters dug in for a federal election June 18, 1962. Here again, as in the provincial vote in 1959, Premier Smallwood vowed to wipe out the Progressive Conservatives. His particular targets were the two sitting PC Members of Parliament, Solicitor General W.J. Browne in St. John's West, and Jim McGrath in St. John's East, whom he accused of betraying Newfoundland. The five other ridings were sure to remain safely Liberal. A former magistrate, Brian White, ran for the Liberals against Jim McGrath but, not surprisingly, McGrath won re-election though with a reduced majority, as the Conservatives were returned to office in a minority government.

To combat Browne, then 65 years old, Smallwood pulled a rabbit out of a hat by announcing the candidacy of Rick Cashin, 25-year-old nephew of Peter Cashin, the firebrand politician most identified with Responsible Government supporters in the Referendum campaigns of 1948. Plastering St. John's West with Richard Cashin posters - there must have been one on every utility pole from city limits to St. Shott's on the southern shore - Liberal campaigners saturated the riding in a seven week blitz. Campaigning personally - a rare action for a provincial Premier in a federal election - Smallwood peppered the electorate with TV and radio ads and personal appearances in Cashin's support. Browne, a seasoned campaigner but lacking the organizational and funding resources and marketing finesse of his opponents, battled to maintain the majority support he had enjoyed in 1957 and 1958. An intense and protracted campaign culminated in a highly dramatic finish. I was there to report for CJON on the voting results:

> It was a tense and often frustrating night for candidates and newsmen at the St. John's West Returning Office. Counts were slow to come in, and even slower in being released for broadcast. And, by the end of the evening, reporters had to rely on unofficial counts, most of them obtained by the candidates themselves from officials or agents whom they had to rouse out of bed.

> The trouble was that some of the deputy returning officers, instead of sending or bringing in their official counts to Returning Officer W.J. Stoyles, failed to do so.

In a few cases, the lists were put into the ballot boxes, while other deputies brought in their boxes, and left again without putting their figures into the hands of the Returning Officer. The result was many delays in compilation of counts, and general confusion as to the reliability of counts that were reported.

Even the first counts did not come through until after nine o'clock, more than an hour after the polls closed, and it wasn't till six hours after polls had closed, at two a.m., that a final count - and that an unofficial one - disclosed Mr. Browne had won the day by the narrow 161-vote margin...Throughout the evening, Mr. Browne was in the Returning Office, scribbling down counts as they were received, and telephoning agents to obtain counts that hadn't been officially reported. He declined to make any comment for broadcast until the final count, saying he preferred not to say anything while the contest was so close. In spite of the closeness of the race, Mr. Browne displayed no outward sign of anxiety over the outcome. Mr. Cashin, who rubbed shoulders with his Conservative opponent throughout the long evening, also remained calm, although the tension of the last several hours was evident in his face, as he waited to see if the final counts could bridge the gap which would mean victory or an agonizingly close second place.

It appears now that Mr. Browne has a clear, although very narrow, plurality, with only one more count, the service vote, to be added in. Returning Officer W.J. Stoyles advised this morning that...the final count for St. John's West (is) 12-thousand, 544 for Browne; 12-thousand, 365 for Cashin, and 273 for Ross. This gives Mr. Browne an edge of 179 votes...Meanwhile, the official count is scheduled for..July 3rd. The law requires that ballot boxes cannot be opened until the official count, and this means, of course, that lists which a few deputies put into their boxes won't be available until that date. But, unless there's been a bad mistake somewhere, it looks like Newfoundland's representation in the new Parliament will be unchanged - Liberals in the five rural ridings and Conservatives in the two St. John's seats. What happens in the next Parliament after this one is anybody's guess.

My strongest recollection of that long night's dramatics was of the glistening tears in the eyes of Rick Cashin as he faced the likelihood of bitter defeat by such a minuscule margin.

Next chapter in this suspense saga came ten days later with the release of service vote results, showing Cashin with a victory over Browne by 39 votes. Polling among service personnel gave Cashin 311 votes as against 102 for Browne and three for NDP candidate Stan Ross. The official count later amended Cashin's lead to 24 votes.

But it did not end there.

Browne submitted a petition to the Supreme Court of Newfoundland to have the election declared null and void because of irregularities in the service vote. He claimed 34 servicemen voted in St. John's West although they listed their residences as outside the riding. In October, separate judgments by Chief Justice R.S. Furlong and Justice H.H. Winter, after hearing evidence presented, declared the election void.

In a provincial election which Premier Smallwood called for Nov. 19, Browne ran and won election in St. John's East Extern. No federal by-election was called, but in a federal general election April 8, 1963, Cashin won handily over Art Harnett, Browne's former executive assistant. All seven Newfoundland seats fell to the Liberals, helping Lester Pearson into power in a minority Liberal government.

PC DOINGS DARK

Much of the frustration involved in dealing with the PC Party of Newfoundland in the 1950's and early 60s stemmed from its chronic ineptitude in communications. Some individuals, of course, were welcome exceptions to this mould - Jim McGrath for instance - but by and large the leading lights of the party shared a debilitating reluctance to speak out plainly, effectively and immediately when circumstances required.

From the unique perspective of a journalist who was also a supporter, this reluctance to communicate was all the more aggravating. Seeking opportunities missed or badly under-used inevitably dampened any enthusiasm to draw out a few nuggets of sage or at least pithy comment to liven up the political scene. Even in the day-to-day routines of journalism, chasing down timely quotes on events and issues of the moment had low to zero success rates. Self-generating statements or comments rarely appeared, and too often quotes that were extracted seldom warranted more than passing notice.

While comments galore would flow from opposition benches during House sessions, utter silence reigned from the Conservative compound throughout the other eight or nine months of the year. Small wonder that terse tributes such as this would surface now and then for pubic attention:

PC Lament

I fear that I will never see
A government of Nfld. PC
So long as politicians sleep
Between elections when they keep
Their doings dark as mystery

PC Annual Meeting 1964

My second journey to Ottawa for a Progressive Conservative Party gathering took place in an atmosphere very different from that prevailing in 1959. The occasion was the annual meeting of the PC Association held Feb. 3-5, 1964. By this time, the bubble of Diefenbaker dominance had long since burst with the party's decline into minority government status in 1962, and defeat at the hands of Lester Pearson in April 1963. Yet the Conservative pow wow was still very much in the news because of a simmering power struggle for leadership of the party.

A sizeable contingent of 28 delegates attended from Newfoundland, led by Opposition Leader Jim Greene and four other House of Assembly members - W. J. Browne and Ank Murphy from St. John's districts, Ambrose Peddle from Grand Falls, and Dr. Noel Murphy from Corner Brook. Others included Jim McGrath, Senator Hollett, Harvey Cole, Bert Butt, Tommy Williams (father of current Premier Danny Williams), Don Parsons, Rex Nichol, Barbara Nugent, Mary Whitten and myself from St. John's, Roy Manuel, Springdale; Ken Twomey, Deer Lake; Mrs. A. Lemoine and Robert MacDonald, Grand Falls; Captain Job Kean, Corner Brook; and H. Osborne, Upper Island Cove; also Art Harnett, then living in Ottawa, as well as spouses of many delegates.

This time, my dual personality status was reinforced as I went with financial support from both CJON Radio/TV and the Newfoundland PC Association. Indeed, a prominent news story in the Feb. 23 edition of the Newfoundland Herald, sported my picture and accompanying story headlined "CJON Covers PC Meet In Ottawa." It read in part:

> CJON Radio and Televison were the only news media in Newfoundland to send a newsman to Ottawa for coverage of (this event). ... Newsman Nix Wadden attended every session of the meeting, as well as some pre-convention meetings, and sent back daily reports by phone, with the emphasis on the part Newfoundland delegates played in the proceedings.... As a result, CJON Radio and TV were able to broadcast fast, accurate reports on what was going on, including:
>
> (1) reaction among Nfld delegates to the leadership issue; (2) details on a resolution on fisheries introduced

at the convention by Mr. W.J. Browne, (3) details of a highlight speech at the convention by 71 year old Capt. Job Kean of Corner Brook; (4) appointment of 25-year old Robert MacDonald as provincial organizer for the PC Association in Nfld.

Leadership Issue

Amid the presentations and discussions on party policies, the underlying issue of party leadership dominated delegates' thoughts throughout the weekend, with intensive lobbying underway by outspoken advocates of holding a secret ballot, and by those who vehemently opposed it. The great majority of the Newfoundland delegates favoured a secret vote, even though most of them strongly supported Diefenbaker's continued leadership. Voting by secret ballot, instead of by an open standing vote, was favoured by some because it would, they felt, serve to forestall any open split within the party ranks. Others argued that a secret ballot would result in a truer picture of the feelings of delegates on the leadership issue. Thus, while most Newfoundlanders at the meeting supported a secret ballot, the majority later voted openly in support of John Diefenbaker as the party leader. The secret ballot proposal was voted down on the convention floor, in a standing vote, by a majority estimated as 10 to 1.

That crucial standing vote posed a "moment of truth" dilemma for me. The overwhelming majority voted in favour, but there were some who, although not voting against, contented themselves with abstaining. Several of the Newfoundland delegation were among the abstainers, and one of them was Jim McGrath, former member of Parliament for St. John's East.

So now, the cat was out of the bag. The simmering disenchantment with Diefenbaker since his disastrous blunders on Term 29 and the IWA strike has taken its toll on party solidarity. For the Newfoundland delegates, the question was what if any impact this split in party unity would have on next election prospects for PC candidates in Newfoundland, especially for Jim McGrath. There was probably good reason to expect that news of this abstention would harm his chances of winning back his St. John's East seat in the next election.

For me, there was a much more basic question: Should I report the fact that McGrath had abstained on this vote, thereby revealing his defection from the fold of Diefenbaker supporters? Part of me - the PC party delegate side - would have preferred not to report on his taking this action, and it could very well have gone unreported since no other media representatives would have noticed, or bothered to report it. So I cannot say that I was not tempted, but sober second thought took over, and I phoned CJON with a full report on the abstention, and its likely significance for McGrath and for the Newfoundland branch of the party. My journalistic conscience was finally clear, even though it made me feel a little like a traitor to the cause.

Yet it took this experience to make me realize that I had been playing with fire for too long, so I vowed because of it never again to play the dual role of delegate and reporter on a political conference. Thereafter, I started to cut down on my PC party involvement, and to distance myself from party functions and personnel. I didn't lose interest, however, and watched events unfold as keenly as ever, but doing so as much as possible at arm's length, as any objective minded journalist should.

As things turned out, disenchantment with Diefenbaker's leadership climaxed with his ouster in 1967. Jim McGrath did not contest the next federal election in 1965, when all seven Newfoundland seats were again won by the Liberals. He was, however, re-elected in 1968, and continued to hold the St. John's East seat until his appointment as Lieutenant Governor of Newfoundland in 1986.

In 1979, when he served as Minister of Fisheries and Oceans in the Joe Clark Government, I had the satisfying experience of directing publicity and communications for the official opening by McGrath of the Northwest Atlantic Fisheries Centre, the new headquarters of the federal Fisheries and Oceans department in St. John's. Working closely with Len Cowley, then DFO regional director general for Newfoundland, and Ed Quigley, regional DFO Information chief, I enjoyed the opportunity to help out a Minister in his own home town.

9
Diversions

FREELANCE VENTURES

Few news people earn so much money that they don't chase after freelance opportunities, and the poorer they are, the harder they look. This was my situation for sure in the early years of married life with a young family, so I picked up whatever extras I could.

Writing for other local publications, such as a magazine or a weekly paper, was fun to do but didn't help much to pay bills, since they seldom could afford to pay for the stuff. One important exception was the monthly Journal of Commerce produced on behalf of the Newfoundland Board of Trade. They did pay, and fairly well for that period of time, when dollar value was a far cry from today's rates.

Publication of the Journal of Commerce was contracted by the Board of Trade to Newfoundland Public Relations Ltd., a company formed in 1959 by a multi-talented trio - Ewart Young, John Maunder and Edsel Bonnell.

Ewart Young will long be remembered as the founding publisher and editor, along with Brian Cahill, of the Atlantic Guardian. Described as a "magazine for Newfoundland", the small format monthly magazine was first published in Montreal in January 1945. Young and the magazine moved to St. John's in 1951, and it continued publication until December 1957. John Maunder was a well known and talented St. John's artist and illustrator.

Ed Bonnell worked as a reporter and news editor at the Evening Telegram, and was publisher and editor of "Here in Newfoundland" magazine published from January to December 1956. He was later to establish his own company, E.J. Bonnell and Associates, which grew into one of the most successful PR and communications firms in the province.

Journal of Commerce

As Journal of Commerce editor, Ewart Young put a lot of story assignments my way, and I surprised myself by getting quite intrigued by the news potential of the commercial world. Writing for the Journal proved a welcome change from the rush rush hurly burly of radio and TV news. Articles needed a certain degree of in depth treatment. Instead of limiting an item to 100 words done fast and furiously for an immediate deadline, here was a chance to explore all facets of a particular subject and to get downright wordy. Given that payment was based on word count - the going rate was 40 cents per column inch - there was lots of incentive to tell the whole story in full detail.

Articles were unattributed - writers were never identified, and that worked fine since there was no need to give our employers the impression that we had too much time on our hands. The range of subject matter was quite broad - covering all facets of the business, commercial and industrial community in the capital city area. I liked the work - getting out to interview business leaders and up and coming entrepreneurs, learning just what it was that they did and how they managed their operations. There were individual profiles to write on local luminaries such as Derrick Bowring, Lewis Ayre, Maurice Wilansky or Harold Luscombe, success stories of new business enterprises, and plenty of newsy notes on current and future events.

Projects which I particularly liked to do were overview reports on entire segments of the economy, such as the fisheries, or the retail trade, or the early inroads of modern marketing. I took special satisfaction in producing, for one issue devoted to communications media, full reports on newspapers, radio and advertising. In so doing I got a chance to compare the sometimes contradictory interpretations by various media representatives of the listening and readership polls on which they based their claims for audience reach. It was fun, while working for one of them, to hear the comments of its greatest rivals. At the same time, I got a better understanding of how they all ticked.

An incidental benefit of earning a few dollars through free lance writing was the discovery of entirely legitimate procedures for saving taxes by offsetting monetary gains with use-of-home and other expenses. My calculations helped but were far too modest. Scanning them years later, it's plain that I could have safely whittled my freelance revenues down to zero without incurring grief from the taxman. Maybe it's a tad late to claim for an adjustment!

Maclean-Hunter

Looking around for likely sources of freelance income, I discovered another promising customer, Maclean-Hunter Business Publications. This Toronto-based organization, an offshoot of which was Macleans Magazine, published an entire "stable" of national magazines devoted to a variety of commercial and industrial sectors. Finding out from friends who already did some work for them, I tracked down the editor responsible for soliciting and editing content from east coast Canada. To my pleasant surprise, it was "Sandy" Campbell, a guy I knew though not very well at St. Francis Xavier University in Nova Scotia, which I attended in 1950-52. He operated out of a branch office in Montreal. As a native Cape Bretoner, he had a tolerably good understanding of the east coast environment, and was quite cooperative and helpful in channelling copy to the various magazine editors.

Magazines like Building Supply Dealer, Canadian Shipping, Home Goods Retailing, Style and Canadian Grocer soon began to take newsy items and the occasional feature. Much of the content involved little research for me because I was already dealing with it in my work for the Journal of Commerce. While the volume was not large, the pay rate wasn't bad - about 3 cents a word, as I remember - so I found it a helpful supplement to my modest income. But I often found myself wondering - what am I doing writing for a little fashion retailing magazine called Style? Wonderful what we can do when we're hungry, isn't it!

Toronto Telegram

A rather more exotic and exciting client for my freelance services was the Toronto Telegram, the swashbuckling enfant terrible of the Toronto media under the aggressive command of John Bassett. Inheriting this gig from a former stringer, I only came up with contributions on a sporadic basis. A few features, such as a rundown on the ravages of the Grand Banks by foreign fishing, caught their eye, and I supplied the odd tidbit on quirky happenings here on the extremities of the nation. They also used reports on the defection of East German sailors from a factory trawler berthed in St. John's.

Undoubtedly the most interesting and at times nerve-wracking assignment I got from the Toronto Telegram occurred in June 1960 and had to do with "the body in the trunk". It started at Argentia when someone checked out a trunk that lay unclaimed and no one knew who was supposed to receive it. It had been sent by rail from Toronto. Opening it at last to find out the contents, officials made the grim discovery of a woman's body. First news reports of the discovery prompted an urgent phone call for me from the Toronto Telegram. Scenting a big story, the Telegram was sending down one of its ace reporters, Frank Drea, and I was asked to guide him around to see what could be found.

Drea, a smart, well experienced reporter wanted to go to Argentia, so I drove him and accompanied him in talking to railway people about the case. As best anyone could judge, Argentia had been chosen as destination for the trunk simply because it was the end of the line on a lightly travelled branch line. Whoever sent it was interested only in getting rid of it for as long a time as possible.

We did quite a bit of dashing around after possible leads - names that cropped up with a potential connection with the victim. His interviews were brief, polite and matter of fact, and he didn't waste time wondering what to do next. Particulars of the case seem to have faded with time, but the positive efficiency and thoroughness of his investigations remain sharply in my memory. In the end, no sensational headline stories were to be found, beyond the initial trunk discovery, but it was a revealing experience to have a few days watching a real investigative reporter at work.

His subsequent career took him from reporting to politics, capped by appointment as a cabinet minister in Bill Davis's Ontario government, covering correctional services, consumer and commercial relations, and community and social services. He was credited with introducing groundbreaking legislation to protect workers and tradespeople, modernize the insurance industry, reform Ontario's prison system and improve the lives of people with disabilities.

Time, etc.

On even rarer occasions, I did a little stringing for one fat cat client, Time Magazine, and even one across the waters, the London Daily Mail. Getting in contact with Time and the Daily Mail arose because my boss at Harvey's News, Ray Simmons, bequeathed them to me when he gave up stringer chores in the mid-1950s. I actually did very little coverage for the Daily Mail, mainly because I found little that interested them which was not adequately covered by the wire services. There was a little more contact with Time, with which I was in any event much better acquainted as a regular reader.

The trouble was that, in the good old days before Confederation, St. John's correspondents for these far off major media had had an exclusive pipeline. Anything that might be earth-shaking in the Newfoundland area - shipping disasters, catastrophic storms, air crashes and the like - rated front page coverage only through despatches from their correspondents. There was no Canadian Press Service in Newfoundland until Confederation in 1949, so there was no competition. Old habits of relying on correspondents persisted beyond 1949, but by the mid-1950s, CP services were now established as the norm, and stringers had to scramble hard and fast to get their stories used.

Commerce Corner

Spending time with, and gaining contacts in, leaders of the business community to fuel stories for freelance customers prompted me, soon after joining CJON, to initiate a business column in its print medium partner, the Nfld. Herald. I called it "Commerce Corner", and turned it into a regular feature which I continued to produce until my departure from CJON, and Newfoundland. Working on that type of content also earned me the designation of Business News Editor for CJON. A sort of honourary title, in effect, but it did facilitate the process of broadening contacts in the business community. Much of the content arose from business contacts and consisted of newsy notes on new stores, interesting new commercial enterprises, and the like.

5-A GOLF AVENUE

After our marriage in June 1959, my wife Madeline and I set up house in a comfortable and enjoyable St. John's apartment at 5A Golf Avenue. It was on the upper floor of a rambling two storey building housing a well known grocery business, the Two Way Stores, and several apartments. Our abode boasted two bedrooms, a large living room with a fireplace, hardwood floors, an old heater and the other usual amenities. A door opened onto part of the roof, flat and protected for use as desired in catching the odd sunrays, or dashing over to visit a neighbouring apartment. The location was even better than we thought as we learned later on. The rent was $90 a month, par for that period. Parking was available on the street outside the door.

I had a spot of a bother at first because the property was owned by G.B. "Bernie" Hefferton, whose brother, Sam, was a Minister in Joey Smallwood's cabinet. And I was no fan of that government. Moreover, Bernie had been in the news not long before this regarding an investigation of alleged skullduggery in his business dealings with government. As it happened, we saw little of him as a rule, since running of the store, and collecting the rents, was handled by his employee, Fred Vail, who was an amiable fellow to deal with. When we did encounter Bernie, he was also personable and treated us properly, so we had no cause for complaint.

We were blessed with friendly neighbours across the roof, Lynn Balsom, an army cook at nearby Buckmasters Field, and his English cockney wife Pauline. He and I teamed up that first year in brewing up a commendably potent batch of beer - he did most of the work. She was a real treat, chatted up a storm and regaled us with a wonderful repertoire of unique sayings that had us in gales of laughter day in and day out. We still guffaw conspiratorially when something reminds us of phrases like "oooah, the styte of me blouse!" or "I'll give you a belt around the air hole", a threat often aimed, but never as far as we know delivered, toward her sometimes grumpy spouse. We missed them terribly when they moved out a year or so later because of a transfer to another army posting.

A neighbour we often saw dashing down the street in early morning had us endlessly puzzled because of his name and his line of work. Trouble was that we could never remember if he was Mr. Barbour, the baker, or Mr. Baker the barber. Never having spoken to the man, the question was never resolved. Had the poor fellow only known, it got to be a regular pastime, speculating idly about Butcher the baker, Barbour the butcher, or Baker the barber. Guess you had to be there. We had to take our entertainment where we could find it in those early days. We took the longest time to get around to buying a TV - it was never important, even though I worked at a TV station.

We looked forward to our first Christmas-New Year's season together as a chance to entertain family and friends, but ran into a real problem. Our oil heater broke down to give us a very cool Christmas, and we had a tough time convincing our landlord to replace it. We had a big party for news media friends lined up for New Year's Eve, and sure enough, it wasn't until that afternoon that the new heater showed up. With guests due at 8:30, the installer only arrived at 6, and it took him three hours to get it working. A lot of inner warmth from the impromptu bar was all that saved us. A good thing, too, since no fewer than four of the spouses, including mine, were pregnant. With so much to celebrate, everyone warmed up very nicely and the party turned out a smashing success. Party-goers included Tony and Sylvia Thomas, Maurice and Ruby Finn, Bill and Margaret Werthman and Gerry and Ruth Bowering. Tony, Maurice and Bill worked at the Telegram, and Gerry was there as a summer replacement reporter soon to begin a teaching career. Joe Dupuis of Canadian Press, recently arrived in St. John's for his two-year assignment, came with a date, but their departure was not without some bother - his car ran out of gas, and they had to hitchhike the rest of the way.

Our apartment's location was great. When I started work at CJON, I was only five minutes away. Then, as Madeline's time for giving birth arrived, she announced that she was going to walk to the hospital. I was aghast, but she had her way, and one fine April morning we strolled along to the hospital door. Fortunately, it was a short route to St. Clare's Mercy Hospital on St. Clare Avenue. All went well, and our daughter, Dianne Marie, was born at 12.45 p.m., ushering in a whole new and exciting phase in our lives.

PARKING WOES

Use of a car when you are a working news reporter has its obvious advantages, but alas also its many hazards. Not the least of these is the ever imminent hazards of breaching the damnably inescapable restrictions on parking. These supposedly petty offences got me in trouble all too often, and once almost landed me in jail.

From the time when I got my first car in 1955 until mid-1959, I drove regularly to work and used the car to get back and forth to VOCM for delivery of news bulletin contents. In so doing, I was often obliged to park as close as possible to the station on McBride's Hill, dashing inside to meet a newscast deadline. There were only two or three places to park on that short hill, and they were usually taken, but there was an area below the big retaining wall which was plainly marked as a No Parking area. So what else was one supposed to do? Time after time, I took a chance by squeezing into that forbidden zone, rushing in to deliver my news package to the third floor studios, and returning as quickly as possible to move my car to a safer, legally approved, haven. Many times that worked, but not always, so all too often I suffered the pangs of finding that nasty ticket tucked under the windshield wiper, and wondering how and when I could pay the fine.

As a consequence, I lived in perpetual fear of parking tickets, and usually with good cause. Payment of parking tickets, and the fines imposed for missing the ticket deadline, became a constant drain on my meagre budget, and gained me little sympathy when I pleaded with traffic enforcers to show me a little slack. True, my generous employers subsidized me to the tune of $20 a month car allowance, but much of this went toward a $60 jump in car insurance, and I'm sure most of the remainder got eaten up in parking fines.

Ruminations on the trauma of too many traffic tickets did, however, produce one snippet of escapist versification that found its way into a dog-eared scrapbook:

One-Way Ticket

No copper: expired!
Then Copper, inspired
No doubt, by promotion,
Slipped ticket on bonnet:
I thought of this sonnet...

When I consider how my cash is spent
(To mention not my patience nor my wrath)
Ere half my bills are paid, not e'en the rent
I'd challenge any cop who crossed my path
And offer him a ticket, yes, in meter,
To show that, basic'ly, I am no cheater!

One copper, as everyone knows, is not worth much...
At best 'tis the price of a match box or some such
At worst 'tis the price that we pay to keep parking,
At least, 'til a copper like you sees the marking...
You'll pardon my saying it, perhaps I'm just tired,
But I wish, for a change, it was you that expired!

Inflation has sure played havoc with that concept - imagine feeding copper pennies into a parking meter nowadays!

The Fort Townshend Fund

It was in a more philosophical mood that I submitted, with covering letter dated Nov. 21, 1959, a traffic fine payment to the court authorities located in an area doubly inimical to motorists for its innumerable potholes as well as its stringent enforcement of traffic laws:

Magistrate's Traffic Court
Fort Townshend
The enclosed cheque to the amount of $22.50 is in payment of fines imposed for traffic violations prior to June 30th, 1959. In forwarding this amount, which I can ill afford, I would like to suggest a worthwhile use to which this money might be put, namely, to lay a proper surface of pavement on Fort Townshend. It has been a source of continual wonder to me how an area that takes in such a substantial proportion of the people's income should be left in such a disgraceful condition. If this suggestion could be passed on to the powers that be, and some action taken, I could feel quite cheerful about parting with my hard-earned $22.50. If not, Sir, I will seriously consider taking my business elsewhere.

Long after, I learned that my sister, Mary Brown, accompanied a traffic payment of hers in that same season with her own wryly phrased lamentations, expressed in verse. Traffic Court officials were so taken with these contributions that they had both pinned for souvenir purposes on the office wall.

Meanwhile, who would have guessed that the potholed ugliness of Fort Townshend about which I then complained was to be outdone a thousand fold nearly half a century later? Traffic ticket square was a thing of beauty compared with the hideous architectural monstrosity of "The Rooms" erected on that site to blot forever the once serene skyline of St John's City.

My Narrow Escape

Accumulating parking fines was far from a laughing matter one frightening morning in August, 1960, when I answered the doorbell at my Golf Avenue apartment to find two strapping members of the Royal Newfoundland Constabulary at my door. They curtly informed me that they were there to collect overdue traffic fines of $85 which I had neglected to pay by the scheduled deadline. When I floundered my excuses and mumbled something about agreeing to come in and settle this up in a few days, they convinced me this was not an option. If I didn't pay the full amount due there and then, they were empowered to take me away and put me under arrest forthwith.

My knees have never been so shaky and my complexion never paler at this frightening prospect, so I cravenly agreed to obey. Keeping them just inside the ground floor doorway, I ran upstairs, snatched up my cheque book, wrote out a cheque for $85, and ran down to thrust it into their hands before they changed their minds. Great was my relief when they accepted the payment, bid me good morning, and went off to chase down some other hapless miscreant.

My plunge into financial despair did not end there, as I still faced one less than minor problem - how was I going to find the money to cover that cheque? It was in between paydays, and my bank account balance was barely perceptible. I could not bring myself to call on my family, so I cast about for a friend to come to my rescue. If I recall correctly, I think I got two friends to contribute enough between them to cover my dangerously-close-to-NSF cheque. After that, I had only two problems to cope with - how to pay each of them back. Well, in time, that too was done, and I could finally relax and enjoy my narrow escape from incarceration. Funny, in a way, how every now and then, I shudder just a tad when I hear that innocent word "fine!"

TRINITY IN '60

News people like everyone else need to get away from it all once in a while, so what better place for that in Newfoundland than Trinity! Madeline and I fell in love with that historic and picturesque haven on our first visit two years earlier. It was late summer 1960, and talk of a long weekend camping trip for six led us back there again.

Our friends, Telegram reporter Tony Thomas and his wife, Sylvia, and Telegram cartoonist Bill Werthman and his wife, Margaret, were enthused as well, so we headed off in two cars for the long jaunt from the city. We and the Thomas's felt a little guilty, since it meant leaving our baby daughters - each only a few months old - behind with grand parents, but they didn't mind in the slightest. The Waddens travelled as passengers with the Werthmans, leaving Bill as driver to find out how bad gravel roads could be once we got off the Trans-Canada Highway. Pitching tents on a camp ground, we enjoyed the pleasures of the open air, though Bill and Tony took time to practise their skills in target shooting.

The community of Trinity itself was tiny by comparison with its surroundings - only a few dozen sturdy homes scattered around a narrow centre. A boat trip within and outside Trinity's shamrock-shaped harbour gave us the opportunity to realize its unique qualities as a hugely spacious sheltered hideaway. It was then not so hard to imagine that, generations ago, as many as 400 sailing ships could shelter here from Atlantic sea swells and enemy encroachments. An endearing mask of shyness by our boatman reflected perhaps a certain discomfort with the influx of strangers among a once proud and self-sufficient people. Notable sights such as Fort Point, guarding the harbour entrance, and big sea stacks popularly christened the Naked Man and the Naked Woman, were duly impressive.

Crowning experience of the weekend for us city folk was a fun-filled adventure in cod-jigging. Incredible as it might appear in the post-moratorium age, cod were clearly plentiful and of quite generous size. Most of us met some success in jigging, but the master, not surprisingly, was Tony, a devoted sports fisherman.

By the shoreline of Trinity we discovered the awesome ruins of the fabled Lester-Garland House, renowned as the oldest residence in Newfoundland. Renowned, perhaps, but ignobly deserted, allowed by property owners and public authorities to crumble helplessly into oblivion. Peeking in through open doors and windows, we could see the skeleton remains of an intriguing circular staircase. Too fragile to tempt one to climb, but strikingly evocate of a long vanished epoch of stately grandeur in what was once a thriving centre of mercantile wealth and industry. Witnessing this tragic symbol of human indifference to the passage of history cast a painful shadow over an otherwise delightful sojourn. Writing about this later in a Newfoundland Herald story, I sadly reported:

> The oldest house in Newfoundland is falling down and nobody is lifting a finger to prevent it from crumbling into oblivion...Unless some authorities awake to the desirability of restoring that valuable relic, tomorrow's visitors will find naught but a heap of dust.

It did not quite come to that as, within a few years of that visit, remnants of the Big House, as some people liked to call it, were torn down. The large brick mansion had been built in the 1760s by merchant Benjamin Lester, and was further extended and refurbished by his grandson, John Bingley Garland, the first speaker in the Newfoundland House of Assembly. It stood as a principal landmark of Trinity Harbour for more than two centuries.

Fund-raising by interested groups in Newfoundland and Britain resulted in reconstruction of the mansion on the same site in 1996-97. Original stone foundations and portions of the end walls were incorporated in the new structure. Apart from a worm-eaten antique table top, it somehow lacks the intrigue and the charm exuded by that mouldering ruin half a century or more ago. It will, however, have to do.

NEWFOUNDLAND WHO'S WHO

A quite unexpected invitation arrived in the mail for me one day in February 1960. The sender, advertising entrepreneur E.C. Boone, advised me that I was included in a "select list of some 300 leaders in civic, church, business, political and social life" which had been carefully compiled by a special Selection Committee. I was, in short, being asked to have my photo and biographical details published in a new "Newfoundland Who's Who". An appropriate form was attached. It would be the first such publication in about ten years.

As flattered as I was surprised, I complied with this request, remarking that I considered it "a mark of honour to the Newfoundland Press Club that you have extended this kind invitation to me in my capacity as President of the Club." And so it was done. I was thereby immortalized on page 73 of the Newfoundland Who's Who, 1961 edition, with this CV summary:

> Wadden, Ronald Nicholas (Nix), B.A. Born August 22, 1930, at St. John's, Nfld., son of Nicholas J. Wadden and Bridget G. Fitzgerald. Educated St. Bonaventure's College, St. John's: Memorial University of Newfoundland; St. Francis Xavier University, Antigonish, N.S. Married. Madeline Roche of St. John's. News Editor VOCM 1957-59. News Editor, CJON November 1959: President, Nfld. Press Club 1958-59; 1959-60. Asst. Secretary, Progressive Conservative Assn. of Nfld 1958-59, 1959-60. Member YPC delegation, Annual Meeting, PC Association of Canada, Nov. 30, 1959; Regional Director of St FX. Alumni Association 1960; Member Knights of Columbus; Memorial University Alumni Assn; 1st St. John's Boy Scout Group Committee; St. Francis Xavier University Alumni Assn.; Newman Club Alumni; Newfoundland Press Club. An organization of press, radio, television, publicity and advertising personnel, the Nfld Press Club promotes community projects and discussion of public issues, and maintains an active social program. Politics: Progressive Conservative. Hobbies: reading and writing. Religion: Roman Catholic. Address: 5A Golf Avenue, St. John's, Newfoundland.

UNTOLD STORY -THE FIRST DEFECTOR

A huge East German fisheries vessel, the Brandenberg, drew scores of curious citizens to the St. John's waterfront when it slipped through the Narrows in July 1961 to tie up along the harbour front. A very rare visitor during that period, it got more than its share of attention a few days later with the news that one of its crew members had jumped ship. The incident was reported by the ship's captain and confirmed by immigration officials. Authorities were advised that Karl Heinz Peters, 23, had left his ship unlawfully, and was still at large. The Brandenberg was one of a fleet of north Atlantic trawlers based at Rostock, East Germany. As days passed, nothing much was reported on the incident, and the trawler headed back to sea without him.

It was weeks later before the missing seaman turned up in public. Yet it was never disclosed where he had been hiding. Until now!

Among citizens gathering to see the big ship on its arrival were two Telegram employees - cartoonist Bill Werthman and reporter Tony Thomas. Bill, who had emigrated to Newfoundland from Germany a decade earlier, got into conversation with Peters when they met along the waterfront, and the three of them became quite friendly. After a while, Peters began talking about how much he would like to move to the West. Then he nervously confided in them that he wanted to jump ship. He said he was tired of living under the East German regime, and wanted his freedom. Yet he was afraid he would be taken back to his ship if he approached local authorities while it was in port. Realizing that the man was serious, the two news colleagues agreed to help him. He managed to take some belongings with him when he left the ship before it sailed.

Thus, over the next week or so, his two new friends took turns in providing shelter for Peters. Tony and his wife, Sylvia, took him into their city home and, for a time, put him up in an out of town family fishing cabin. He also spent some time with Bill and Margaret Werthman at their home in Mount Pearl. As a Telegram reporter, Tony was able to keep tabs on any efforts made to search for the defector. Meanwhile, wheels were set in motion to have his case put before immigration authorities.

Throughout this lengthy process, the newspaperman in Tony must have been bursting to tell the story of what was happening, but he resisted the temptation, concerned more for ensuring the seaman's security than for the chance to score a journalistic coup. Ironically, it was Tony's colleague at the Telegram, columnist Don Morris who, three months later, broke the intriguing follow-up story on its repercussions back in East Germany. Mention was made of the role played by local residents, but their names were not disclosed.

In his column Oct. 10, Morris reported that the East German newspaper "High Seas Fisherman" cited Peters' case in accusing "NATO spies and enemies of the East German republic" of luring seamen away from their ships in western seaports. The paper claimed that "enemies" were using six methods of luring fishermen from their vessels (1) bribery (2) empty promises (3) promises with only "10 to 75 percent truth in them" (4) distribution of certain articles like liquor, food, 'southern fried chicken', women who were "colleagues or secretaries" of those trying to lure them away (5) employment of psychology such as "pity" for the seaman because he does not have the same good things which people have in the west (6) showing the seaman new houses, new developments and urging him to leave "the old way" and come to live in the west. To combat these temptations, special committees were being set up on ships of the East German fishing fleet to impress upon seamen that enemies of the East German republic were operating in NATO ports.

Karl Peters' side of the story was that he was tired of living under the restrictions of the East German Communist regime. Over there, he said, life was hardly worth living. His home city was drab and the people were unhappy, and he wanted to live in freedom in the west. A St. John's lawyer took up the case and federal Cabinet Minister W.J. Browne requested the immigration department to give it top priority. This was done, and he was eventually granted political asylum. He found employment in St. John's and eventually moved into his own apartment. I met Karl Peters a number of times at the Werthmans' home in Mount Pearl. He appeared well satisfied with his new life. It must have agreed with him since, the last I heard, he was still living near St. John's.

BRISTOL'S HOPE - THE LIGHT ON THE HILL

Can't really believe it, but the evidence is here before me - a news item complete with my picture on my taking a vacation! "CJON Newsman Taking Off for Holidays", the headline proudly announces. It is of course the Newfoundland Herald, Sep. 9, 1962 edition, and it's doing what comes naturally in promoting the activities of a staff member of its sister medium, CJON. The story goes like this:

> It's getting near the end of the annual vacation period in the CJON newsroom with the final news editor to take his holiday being Nix Wadden. Nix has been hard at work all the summer but does not feel too badly about his colleagues getting their vacation early...at least this year. It poured rain all the summer and now Nix is hoping to get some of the sunshine which passed us by during the regular vacation period. Nix is not saying where he will be during the three weeks but has given notice that he will be miles away from a telephone. Incidentally during his absence, the popular "Commerce Corner" which he writes for the Nfld Herald will not be published. The column will be back in the usual spot in mid-September.

Sure enough, Commerce Corner did return Sep. 21, not to trumpet the wondrous exploits of the mercantile world, but to offer a report card on a unique "Vacation Interlude."

> Having been away from the desk for a couple of weeks vacation, and a rather unique one at that, it's a shame to clutter a whole column of commercial comments without some reference to holiday experiences. Especially as this particular vacation was very much of a non-commercial nature. It's also an opportunity to reply to Jack Howlett's recent expressions of disenchantment with his trip to the "Boston states".
>
> To begin with, one can scarcely rhapsodize about the joys of electric appliances - of "living electrically" - after spending a few weeks cut off from electric power. The place we chose to while away our holidays was the picturesque Conception Bay community of Bristol's

Hope, a tiny coastal settlement hidden away all to itself between Carbonear and Harbour Grace. It has no electricity and, judging by the scattered location of its few families, precious little hope of getting same. As visitors, of course, we were only too pleased to find ourselves lighting up the venerable oil lamp (it was supposed to burn kerosene, but stove oil proved just as good.) A Coleman lamp lent by a kind friend made us, indeed, the envy of the valley. There was no electric stove, no electric boiler, no television, and, best of all, no telephone. Only a transistor radio to remind us of the outside world, and even that rested silently for many an evening. It was, in a word, just glorious.

It takes an experience such as that - living a while, no matter how brief - in a small, neighbourly Newfoundland community, to realize this island still retains its genuine-ness, its unspoilt humanity, its hospitality. Our nearest neighbours, Bob Butler and his Mrs., couldn't do enough for us, providing water (our well was dry), homemade bread, a mouth-watering salt beef and cabbage dinner, and even blueberries. If there's anything a trueborn "townie" hankers for whenever he's "in the country", it's a brimful jug of fresh-from-the-cow milk, or fresh butter, eggs, and scald cream, the good things that once flowed so plentifully but nowadays seem to be increasingly rare. How downright tragic it sounded when another neighbour, Mrs. Harris, confessed that she has to throw away milk by the gallon, for want of someone to take it.

It is in these good things of the earth and the homestead that Newfoundland's singular character is to be found. Healthy food, healthy air, and hospitable people can be the staple product this island offers the tourist, whether he be from St. John's or San Francisco. In such vital and genuine communities as Bristol's Hope, Newfoundland has more to offer the stranger than he can ever repay.

That column did not nearly do it justice, but space was limited, so that had to do for the Herald. In fact, that simple sojourn remains one of our fondest of all memories of Newfoundland. For my wife, Madeline and me, the Bristol's Hope experience provided a change from our usual vacation pattern of driving to Gander to visit relatives in their modern homes in a modern town - we both had sisters living there. Moreover, as apartment dwellers in St. John's, we wanted to see what it was like to live for two weeks in a home to ourselves.

The very name, Bristol's Hope, drew us to explore its attractions. That, and its fabled renown as the home of the first recorded birth in Newfoundland. As the story goes, a daughter was born here in the early 1600s to Irish Princess Sheila na Gueira and Gilbert Pike, a former shipmate of the infamous pirate, Peter Easton. Some doubt about those details, but it's a great legend anyway.

Our holiday haven in Bristol's Hope was a sprawling two-storey homestead perched on the side of a high hill overlooking the valley. Down through it flowed a narrow stream emptying into a snug little cove that in earlier days used to be called Mosquito. Our two-year-old daughter, Dianne, called it our Holiday House - though that came out more like "holly house," and she hated to be away from it. Like us, she lost her heart to what she called "Brissels Hope." Our friendly next door neighbour, she called "Missila Butler." We rented the house from the property owner in Harbour Grace. It was a fine sturdy dwelling, and wasn't very old, having been built only about 25 years earlier, but there had been no one living in it for the last six years. It was surrounded by a sturdy fence, and had what used to be a wonderful garden, with all kinds of plants, fruit trees and flowers, though now much overgrown or gone partly to seed.

We were duly warned about the home's supposed deficiencies. It had no lights, no running water, no indoor toilet, no telephone, no television, no modern range or kitchen facilities. Furnishings were sparse. On the ground floor, just a battered old King Edward coal stove, rusty chimney funneling, a table, a rocking chair, an old stuffed chair, half a dozen home made kitchen chairs and, best of all, a settle. Upstairs, the master bedroom where we slept had a big high bed, reasonably comfortable and piled with blankets and fluffy pillows. No heat, but for a young couple that was no problem. For us, the whole place was just perfect!

The homestead had been well preserved since its last permanent resident moved out. The bright floral pattern wallpaper could have been put on a few months earlier instead of maybe 10 years or so. True, the doors were warped so that few closed properly, but we had no fear of unwelcome visitors. At night, we set the Coleman lantern on a picnic table outside, and often read by its light after dinner was done and our daughter put to bed. That lantern cast its brilliant light rays out over the river valley - so much so that community residents whom we met on our daytime wanderings remarked how brightly it shone way up there on the hill.

And thereby hangs a lovely flashback tale. More than 20 years later - in the summer of 1985 - Madeline and I returned to Bristol's Hope to look for our holiday house, and had trouble finding it. Stopping along the road to ask a local fisherman, Robert Taylor I think was his name, we tried to explain whereabouts it was, but couldn't remember the family name of the owners, or the laneway on which it stood. Then, out of desperation, we mentioned the Coleman lantern.

"Ohhh yes," says he, his eyes wide as saucers, "I minds that light! You could see it all over the valley." So he told us how to get up there, and we made it. Only to find it a sad and ghostly remnant of that fine old homestead. The house was gone completely, leaving barely the outlines of the foundation. Fragments of concrete pillars were all that was left of the entrance gateway. Garden flowers and plants were totally overgrown, lost in wild and nondescript brush skirting the overall property. Only the bright and happy memories remained.

Dianne and Madeline on "holly house' doorstep (Nix Wadden photo)

THE PAVING OF MOUNT PEARL

October 1962 brought on a new phase in my family's life as we left our cozy Golf Avenue apartment in St. John's to move into a smaller and decidedly less comfortable flat in Mount Pearl. The move was made for a simple practical reason - it was cheaper to rent. Dropping from $90 to $60 a month was a welcome relief for me after months of struggling to keep up with bill payments in the city. And we had started saving for a down payment on a house of our own.

We were on the ground floor of a bungalow at 214 Park Avenue, seven miles by my count from CJON, but gas prices were pretty low in those days, so the drop in rent made it a lot easier to make ends meet. The accommodations were not lavish - just two bedrooms, living room, kitchen and bathroom, and an oil heater, but no fireplace.

Our landlord and lady - Charlie White and his spouse, Edith - lived beneath us with their daughter, Brenda, who was about the same age as our Dianne, and they played together quite a bit. A mother and her son lived in another apartment one floor above us.

It was not very long before we learned something we didn't much care to hear about our hosts - horror of horrors - he was a cousin of our worthy Premier, J.R. Smallwood. So we'd done it again - committed non-admirers of the Liberal leader, for the second time living in a place owned and run by people closely connected to him.

Such unwelcome considerations dimmed considerably in importance as we got to know and like our downstairs hosts/neighbours, and learned the benefits of tolerance and good will as against mindless prejudice. Though we never became great friends, we got along quite well throughout our stay.

One expression Charlie mentioned one day in musing about what might be termed the Mount Pearl mentality stuck with me: People around here, he said, are afraid of each other. He didn't mean physically afraid, but rather inhibited and unwilling to become truly open and friendly toward each other, as people used to behave in typical Newfoundland communities. The fact that Mount Pearl was a dormitory town - everyone working somewhere else - doubtless had much to do with it. Certainly we too sensed that cold reserve feeling which we had not been used to back in the city.

Car troubles dogged us quite a bit in Mount Pearl, and calls for help from a nearby garage were frequent. Charlie did his share of tinkering to try and help us, and he so frequently intoned a verdict on the source of our troubles. "It's all" he said, "in the timing." And, you know, more often than not, that's what the garage man concluded as well. Neither succeeded in fixing it on a permanent basis, but the message was not forgotten. Even nowadays, many many kilometres from Mount Pearl, whenever engine trouble rears its ugly head, we look at each other, sagely nod our heads, and mutter "It's in the timing."

We had been going to Mount Pearl often before moving in there, as we had become great friends with the Werthman family. Bill Werthman worked for a number of years as the Telegram cartoonist, and demonstrated his skills as an artist in various ways and on various projects. One topic on which we had long agreed was the deplorable state of road surfaces in the community. We were not alone. Although the roadway we lived on, Park Avenue, was paved, it was the only one in the town that was not plagued with dust and potholes.

Road conditions were a natural topic for attention when election time rolled around. By happy coincidence, I was in Mount Pearl one Saturday morning when an election entourage roared into town. It was Premier Smallwood himself, speaking through a loudspeaker mounted outside Samson's Supermarket. The date was March 30, 1963, just a week before a crucial federal election, and Joey had something big to announce. His statement, text of which I scribbled down as he delivered it, was short and, to the voters of Mount Pearl, particularly sweet:

> This is Premier Smallwood speaking, and I have the Liberal candidate for St. John's West, Richard Cashin, with me. I have come here today to make two very important announcements... You will be very glad to hear them. First, you have in your town today six and half miles of streets and roads not paved. (One and a half miles are paved on Park Avenue.) If we have a Liberal victory on the 8th of April, if we have a Liberal government in Ottawa, two or three days after that victory the Newfoundland government that I'm the head of will call for tenders from contractors to place a contract to pave every street and road in Mount Pearl-Glendale, to let the contract this spring to have work start this summer.
>
> Second, electricity. You are customers of United Towns. You pay higher rates than you would if you were

customers of Nfld. Light and Power. Can anything be done about that? Could we put United Towns out and put Nfld Light and Power in? No, we cannot. United Towns has a franchise given 50 years ago. Could we lower your rates? Yes. Yesterday I sent for the chairman of the power commission... and I instructed him to bring in a plan whereby the power commission will pay the difference between the two rates. You'd' pay the same as Nfld. Light and Power rates...It would only cost $35,000 a year to the power commission.

A great Liberal victory on Monday week and every street and road in your town will be paved by the Newfoundland government. And the government will pay for every cent of that cost, not the town council, the government. That will be the result of a great Liberal victory on April 8th.
The Liberal government have agreed to pay 90 per cent of the Trans Canada Highway. With Ottawa paying 90 cents of every dollar, the Newfoundland government will save millions and millions of dollars, and this is what will give us the money.

I ask you to give the biggest Liberal majority ever...and if you do, you'll have good reason to be very very happy people. This is a lovely town, but what it lacks, what it doesn't have, are paved roads and streets...Give us a great Liberal victory and you'll be happy people you did.

Within minutes after this speech, I dashed home and phoned the story in to CJON, which broke the news as an exclusive - there were no other reporters on the scene. Needless to say, the story caused quite a stir - prompting sharp attacks by Conservatives and editorial writers incensed by what they saw as the Premier's latest example of bribing the voters.

Conservative candidate Art Harnett did what he could to stem the tide. Campaigning in Mount Pearl two days before the polls closed, he stressed the fact that he, unlike his opponent, could stand on his own two feet. "Last week, the Liberal candidate was in here to Mount Pearl. But nobody heard a word from him. The talk all came from Premier Smallwood. Little Ricky just kept his mouth shut, and did as he was told..." Pointing out that similar paving and other promises had been made but not kept in past elections, however, had little impact. Cashin swept the riding by a 3,000 vote majority as all seven Liberal candidates rolled on to help defeat the Diefenbaker government and bring Lester Pearson to power.

Watching the paving machines roll into action in the following year, I felt a little tremor of satisfaction. Would this have happened at all, I wondered, if I had not been on the scene that day near Samson's Supermarket. I like to think that my putting the story on the air made this one promise that Joey Smallwood just had to keep.

I Owe It All To Neddy

Among my youthful contemporaries, I was a real late comer to the tempting evils of smoking. While many of my school mates were puffing away at 12 and 13, I only managed one quick sample and that turned me off for years. So great was the pull of peer pressure, however, that on one or two occasions I offered to contribute to their ill gotten pleasures by buying a package of Flags. That was the brand name of the cheapest, foulest smelling variety of cigarette churned out by the Imperial Tobacco Factory. A dark foreboding high walled edifice at Bond and Flavin Streets, the "backer" factory as I used to call it as a small kid, was just the source - sales were made at any of the small neighbourhood stores for a hefty ten cents a pack. So I bought them, but gave them all away.

Wariness of the weed stayed with me until about my second year at university, and, even at that, I indulged only occasionally. Working outdoors in summer highway survey jobs had its special moments of sheer pleasure, resting under leafy birches to enjoy a cooling smoke break near the end of the day. It was another summer job - toiling indoors at the mind-numbing task of drafting and re-drafting organization charts for the U.S. Air Force - that got me into a little more serious smoking. Lighting one fag after another, only to let most of them burn away in ash trays - meant that I was hooked at last. Early favourites, because they were cheap at the base canteen, were Camels, but I gradually turned to slightly milder stuff like Export A. Consumption usually stayed within a pack a day but, with a young family, I begrudged the drain on my pocket.

Doing serious news work was a smoker's natural milieu, it seemed, since everyone indulged, and it went so well with after-hours beer drinking so popular with the newsy set in those days. Of course everyone grumped and groaned about it, vowing always to quit the stuff, but seldom making real effort to do so. Desire to break the habit began to hit home, finally, with a young daughter around the house and the prospect of a further family addition. But how to do so? Simple overnight pledges to cut down and cut out got nowhere. Something else was needed.

That's where Neddy came in.

Hon. Edward S. Spencer, Minister of Finance, as he was then - about 1964. His budget presentation that year included a gratuitous gift to the cause of better health and fewer nasty habits by imposing a five cent increase in the provincial tax on a pack of cigarettes. Well, if ever one wanted a good reason to quit the weed, that was it. That very day, I resolved to put an end to smoking. And I got immediate close support - my wife Madeline decided to join me.

The first few hours were easy but, after that, resolution slipped a mite, and by next day, we had weakened enough to grasp a few more puffs. OK, we decided, let's do it this way - see how long we can go without smoking, and only give in when we can't stand it another minute. That worked not too badly, as we made it smoke free for more than half a day. Next, we set a definite goal - to go 24 hours without a cigarette. It was maybe the 3rd or 4th day that we realized we'd done it. And I've never looked back - that was the end of my smoking career. Madeline actually made it too at the same time, but slipped back into the habit some years later when there was a death in the family. The lapse didn't last too long, and she kicked the habit for good without too much trouble.

There, for what it's worth to anyone, is our simple formula for saying goodbye to smoking. Get off it for 24 hours, and you've got it made. Easy? No, but it worked for us.

And it is so cool to be able to say - as I just love to do when confronting any hardened nicotine-stained wretch I meet -"No, I don't smoke. I gave it up when cigarettes went from 35 to 40 cents a pack!"

Bless you, Neddy Spencer!

10

CJON Radio & TV

CJON - A New Beginning

Going to work for CJON was very much a mixed blessing for me. It gave me a job, of course, and that was rather important, just five months after getting married and with apartment rent and expenses to pay for. Yet it was hard to swallow after working for five years to make VOCM its closest news competitor. It was akin to crossing the floor from the opposition to the government side, and I felt a bit guilty about it.

It was, moreover, taking a step backward, since it meant going from a position as head of one news organization - a news director in all but name - to becoming just another news editor in a group of half a dozen reporting to the CJON news director. It would be a relief to shed those management responsibilities, but I'd miss the good things that went with running an operation.

It had, however, its own rewards, since I was now working with a pretty able and friendly bunch of guys - no girls yet - with an amiable, competent boss, news director Jim Thoms, and many new things to learn. Around the U-shaped newsroom desk we sat together. My new colleagues included Burn Gill, Jim Quigley, Jack Howlett, George Perlin, Bill Callahan and Wally Millman. I had known or at least met most of them before, and of course Jack Howlett had worked with me at Harvey's and VOCM. This group produced an imposing volume of news, supplying CJON radio newscasts on the hour every hour of the day between 6 a.m. and midnight, and also CJON television news at noon, 6 p.m. and 11 p.m. Much of the news content for TV was lifted straight from the radio news, but original text was needed for stories involving the use of film or videotape clips.

Only a month or so after I joined CJON, I found myself in a most unusual role for me - as a sort of a stand up comedian. The station was having its Christmas party, and the entertainment for the evening, apart from some dancing and carousing, was to be supplied by staff members doing their thing, whatever it was. My first reaction on being asked to take part was to decline, since I was new anyway and hadn't done any singing since boy scout days. Then, on the spur of the moment, I changed my mind and said: Why not?

Thus, lo and behold there I was in front of a microphone, dressed hobo-ish with a plaid shift and a knotted pair of braces, telling a silly story, and singing an old boy scout song. My little story told of my confusion about the CJON hierarchy, on the one hand, and a pop group that was currently all the rage, the Four Js. The thing was that, from the moment I came in the door at CJON, I kept hearing about "Mr. J.", and wondered who that was until I realized they were talking about the boss, Don Jamieson. Then I pointed out that we also had "Mr. Colin", Don's brother who was CJON sales manager. And there was also an even younger brother, commonly known as "Dubie", who worked as a technician. So, I wondered, where was the fourth "J"? (Little did I know at the time, and there was a fourth brother, Bas ("Dat You Baz"), who was not involved in CJON in those years.)

The story got a laugh, anyway, so I finished up by singing my little ditty about a tramp's favourite refrain:

> Rock me to sleep on a clothes line
> Hang up me bowler to dry
> Tuck me in purple pyjamas
> And then let me curl up and die!

One new thing for me in the CJON news setting was the necessity of doing shift work, since news editors needed to be on the job between 6 a.m. and midnight seven days a week. The more senior types - Jim Thoms and Burn Gill - were on day shift only, but the rest of us had to take turns on morning shifts - 6 a.m. to 2 p.m. - day shifts 9 a.m. to 6 p.m., and night shifts - 6 p.m. to midnight. It all worked out to five days out of seven, and about 35 hours a week.

The weekly cycle would include a combination of all three, but since we had to cover weekends as well, this could be a little irregular. The good thing was that every three weeks we could get four days off in a row. Moreover, the system was flexible enough to let us choose to work a night shift and morning shift back to back, giving us a longer break before the next three days of our week on duty. In a typical week, I might work a Saturday night and 9 to 6 Sunday, be off Monday and Tuesday, and then go back on various shifts Wednesday to Friday.

Working that night shift - by yourself after about 7 p.m. - meant that you seldom left the station before 1 a.m., so that, if you had talked yourself into doing the morning shift the next day, you had to be back in by 6 a.m. - with about four hours sleep to keep you going. This didn't happen often, but when you got used to it, it wasn't so hard, and you got the benefit of a few days off before checking back in.

Night shift work had its share of headaches but also some welcome diversions. Apart from the brief hourly radio newscasts, there was the late night local news on television, which always called for special attention. And then there was the DOSCO news, the 15-minute radio news program sponsored by the Bell Island mining company and catering to audiences in Conception Bay and rural areas generally. Styled in some ways like the Gerald S. Doyle News Bulletin, it was a pot pourri of folksy information.

As regular as clockwork, one of the notices phoned in for the DOSCO called for a meeting of the International Association of Bridge, Structural and Ornamental Iron Workers of America, local number 764, to be held at 3 p.m. Sunday at Conception Harbour. This was the union headquarters for all of those doughty Newfoundlanders who made their living journeying to New York and other big U.S. cities to work on the high steel girders used in the construction of skyscrapers. Yet, somehow, I can't think of the DOSCO news without remembering the story written for it a few years earlier by Charlie Bursey about the passing of a man who, he reported, has been mortally wounded in the first world war.

A constantly cheerful and friendly person, Charlie Bursey and I crossed paths frequently in those years. We probably first met when he was a news editor at CJON from 1953 to 1957. He spent some time working for the Progressive Conservative Party, as I did at a later time. We worked closely together on the Press Club executive. He was at the Doyle Bulletin from 1958 to 1963, then went into public relations with Newfoundland Light & Power. Then in 1966, he became the federal Fisheries Information Officer in St. John's. His later career included public relations stints with ALCAN, BRINCO, CFLCo, and Nfld. Hydro.

Working that early morning shift at CJON could also have its compensations. One morning, when I had barely tumbled out of bed on time to dash into the station for my 6 a.m. start, I got a welcome surprise. Burn Gill, who as a senior editor worked 9 to 6 weekdays, dropped on my desk just before 9 a piping warm dish of bacon and eggs. "You always look hungry on these morning shifts," he said. "Eat up." So I did. The gesture, coming from a guy noted for his gruff and aggressive manner, was most unexpected, but he repeated it many times afterwards. Living only a few streets from the station, he carried the "hot plate" on his walk to work. It was a memorable mark of kindness for which I was always grateful.

Burn went on, like so many other news colleagues of those days, to greater things, building the Newfoundland Archives into a remarkably successful service. He was the provincial archivist from 1969 to 1979, and was honoured when the province gave his name to the Records Management Centre in Pleasantville. In his earlier days he served for seven years with the Newfoundland Ranger Force, was editor of the Corner Brook Western Star and City Editor of the St. John's Daily News before joining CJON in 1960.

Jim Thoms proved an effective leader in the newsroom, having a keen eye for subjects and stories to catch the public's attention. Serious minded and hard working, he had succeeded Bren Walsh as news director in 1956, and continued in the job until the early 70s, when he moved on to other things. A former teacher, he started at CJON Radio in its opening year, 1951. A longtime admirer of Premier Smallwood, he took up book editing for the Premier, as associate editor of Books Three and Four of the Books of Newfoundland, and served as editor of the government newspaper, the Newfoundland Bulletin. He went on to become Editor of the Daily News, serving from 1971 until the last edition rolled off the presses in June 1984. He capped his remarkable career by moving on to CJON-TV's successor, NTV, in 1985, putting in another 15 years.

Bill Callahan had been with CJON since 1952 and when I arrived he was mainly dealing with sports news, so we didn't work closely together. He left for the Western Star about the time when I started.

George Perlin only worked at CJON for about a year after I arrived, as he went on to academic studies at Queen's University in Kingston, Ont. in 1960. He was a likeable colleague - I'll always remember his carefree demeanour on a blustery, blizzardy night when he drove me home from CJON through knee deep snow drifts. He told me recently he too remembers that night - he drove afterward to his parents' home and couldn't see the driveway, so he plowed the car into a snowbank, "and next morning, no sign of it!" And then there was the time - one I was reminded of by another friend of that era - when, doing a sports news broadcast which he did on occasion, he blithely began: "Good evening, George Perlin, This is ladies and gentlemen."

A good newsman with a sharp eye for political news in particular, he had also worked at VOCM, and at the Daily News, to which he returned for some time later before settling down to the academic life. In 1968, after completing his studies, he took on the role of Daily News Publisher, but resumed his academic career a year or so later. Ever interested in politics, George specialized in political science studies, launching a successful and high profile career as a national polling expert and Professor of Political Science at Queen's. Since retirement, he has remained active as Emeritus Policy Studies Professor and founding director of the Queen's Centre for the Study of Democracy.

Wally Millman had one distinguishing talent among newsroom staff - he was by far the best typist of the lot, turning out letter perfect copy that must have been a joy to all news readers. Many if not most of us were self taught fumble fingered keyboard amateurs by comparison. Laying no claim to being one of the best writers, Wally yet managed to turn out his share of newscast copy as needed. Being of an upbeat and outgoing personality, he found his forte in taking on outside broadcast assignments, ably handling on site interviews on a variety of topics.

Through the next few years, some new faces such as Bill Bown and Larry Rossiter appeared in the newsroom. Summer replacements of note included Ed Roberts, fresh from a two year stint as Editor of Varsity, the University of Toronto student newspaper, while he was preparing for law studies. Competent and occasionally caustic, as young university tyros tend to be, Ed fitted in well with his demonstrated writing talents and thorough understanding of public affairs and politics. It was no big surprise when he emerged a few years later as Executive Assistant to Premier Smallwood, and eventually an MHA and cabinet minister. I was pleased to receive from Ed in the mid-70s a letter congratulating me on an Information Services promotion in the Fisheries and Oceans department. Guess I owe him one for his making it all the way to Lieutenant Governor.

Broadcasting Personalities

CJON announcers were a pretty good lot too. John Nolan did the flagship 1:15 p.m. Blue Star News, and would pop in to chat and glance at the content during the morning. With his blonde haired good looks and flamboyant personality, I wasn't too sure if I liked him at first, especially as he often came in carrying the latest Playboy magazine under his arm. However, he surprised me by talking a lot about the serious articles written in between those blowsy babe foldouts, so he had a good mind behind all that facade. His subsequent career as a politician, cabinet minister and citizenship court judge amply demonstrated that. And he was a really nice guy all around.

He did have one quirk, however, that we in the newsroom learned to watch out for, and avoid if we could. John had an aversion to reading out long foreign names, and unfailingly applied his own solution to the problem - he'd skip them over. Thus, if the story was about a visit from the Secretary of State, M. Gérard Pelletier, he would read "..the Secretary of State", slide effortlessly past the name, and so on. If the next sentence began "Mr. Pelletier.." he would either mumble the name unrecognizably or just say "he", and carry on. Whenever we could, we'd omit the name too, but that wasn't always possible, so it was a case of having to grin and bear it as he ploughed on unphased.

Funniest memory I have of John Nolan was his telling about squirming around one day in a remote broadcast booth set up for reading the noon time TV newscast. There was no technician-operator on hand - the whole process was fully automated . He just had to face the camera and read the news he held in his hands. Only problem was that this time, the pages slipped out of his grasp onto the floor below. Sweating profusely, he had to squeeze and squirm around as best he could, stretching an arm out as far as he could reach to retrieve the lost pages without letting the TV audience know what was happening. How he did it, he never knew, but he did manage to clutch at least some of the pages and finish what he would long remember as the newscast from hell.

Bob Lewis was the station's star radio "personality", renowned for his golden voice and always pleasant approach to people. An American who served in the U.S. Air Force at Pepperrell, married a Newfoundland girl, and settled in St. John's, he was seldom recognized by his real name, Clarence Engelbrecht. He later served as a member of the City Council. Charlie Pope, whom I had first encountered when he played goal for Prince of Wales hockey team, and I was goalie for St. Bon's, did regular announcing duties for some years before moving on to become radio sales manager. Art Andrews was another popular broadcast personality in those CJON days. He later moved on, I believe, to CBC. In more recent years, Art devoted increasing attention to his home community of Trinity, operating a number of business enterprises, including a bed and breakfast at Trinity East in which we spent a pleasant vacation visit in 2000.

One interesting member of the broadcast staff who took more than passing interest in news activities was Gerry Ottenheimer. A jolly exterior combined with keen intelligence made him a welcome intruder. His subsequent career took him for a few years to Memorial University as film studies supervisor and then into politics. Just after I moved from St. John's to Ottawa early in 1966, I chanced to meet him one day and drove him around the capital area. He was elected to the House of Assembly that year, going on to become Opposition Leader and in later years a cabinet minister, Speaker of the House and a Senator. I'm not sure when this was but I well recall one occasion when we met in Halifax airport. My feet almost got sore that day as he walked me back and forth from one end of that large terminal to the other, talking all the time of Newfoundland affairs past and present.

Gerry Wiggins was another outstanding presence among CJON news personalities. The big smiling new arrival from Toronto took little time to make himself known to his listeners as CJON circulated a postcard, inviting the public to see how many times they could write "Gerry Wiggins" on that card. The count was in the several hundreds, but the impact was instant success for this simple PR ploy. He got into lots of activities, even the CJON bowling league, and earned a widespread following for his radio and TV shows. More success came when he ran for a City Council seat, as he served citizens well until he was felled prematurely by cancer. The outpouring of public grief on his passing was quite remarkable.

Clark Todd, an announcer from New Brunswick, appeared to be settling down when he married a CJON switchboard operator but the magic did not last, and they split up. Although he showed interest in the news, it was a surprise to see that he developed into a successful television reporter and foreign correspondent when he moved to England. He was the CTV London bureau chief when he was killed in September 1983 while covering a bitter conflict in Lebanon. He was honoured with a posthumous Michener Award "to recognize an unusual individual whose efforts exemplify the best in public service journalism." A two-hour made-for-TV movie "War Correspondent - the Clark Todd Story" was presented on CTV to mark his achievements.

Howie Meeker spent a lot of time at CJON, doing a regular physical education kind of show as well as sports, with the emphasis on hockey. He succeeded Bill Callahan as Sports Editor in 1959. Howie had his hand in various business enterprises, especially in the construction and operation of bowling alleys. He was a gregarious guy, always happy to chat with everyone and argue in a friendly way about anything. He built a fine house at St Phillips and often entertained co-workers who came by for a visit. He moved to B.C. in the mid 60s.

Ken Meeker, Howie's younger brother, was hired at CJON and worked on the newsroom staff for several years. He later moved on to CBC.

John Carter joined the newsroom staff in 1963 after spending three years at VOCM. He later worked as a news editor at the Telegram before opening his own public relations business.

CJON's, and Newfoundland's, first television news cameraman was Nelson "Nels" Squires. I worked with him fairly often, and found him to be one of the best news photographers in the city. His newspaper background was mainly at the Telegram though he had earlier worked at the Daily News. His move to CJON came after it got its TV licence in 1955, and he was for the next decade the photographic mainstay of the station's news operations.

Covering TV news stories with Nels and his camera was always a pleasurable experience. Not only was he a very friendly and cooperative individual, but he was also a skilled photographer with a natural instinct for getting just the right kind of shot or sequence needed for the evening news. There was no backup staff to work with - we used to wonder at the sheer number of bodies involved when CBC TV sent in a crew on the same story that our twosome looked after quite nicely on our own. Their cameramen such as Frank Kennedy and John O'Brien were highly skilled as well, drawing also on many years in newspaper photography, and maybe we wouldn't have minded getting those extra hands to help us, but we managed to cope quite well anyway.

Nels was given a big farewell party at the Newfoundland Hotel when he left the station in March 1965 to open his own photographic studio. A presentation on behalf of the staff was given to him by Howie Meeker. After operating his studio for a couple of years, Nels went to work for the Film and TV unit at Memorial University.

TV LICENCES FOR NEWFOUNDLAND

In "The Swashbucklers", his account of broadcasting wars between the CBC and private broadcasters, former national CBC news and public affairs director Knowlton Nash devotes a lot of attention to the role played by Don Jamieson.

> Private broadcasting won another victory with the granting of a TV licence for St. John's in 1955. The CBC board of governors had recommended a CBC station be established in Canada's easternmost city. Its second choice was a licence for CJON St. John's, run by Don Jamieson and his partner, Geoff Stirling. It was up to the cabinet to make the final decision and, the CBC thought, give its blessing to the public broadcaster. But Jamieson's close friendship with Jack Pickersgill, who was now in the cabinet as secretary of state, and with the Liberal premier of Newfoundland, Joey Smallwood, paid off.

> The two Newfoundlanders flew to Ottawa to lobby senior Liberals. They met with Pickersgill, among others, and, on their behalf, Pickersgill argued in cabinet that a CBC outlet in St. John's would be a waste of taxpayers' money when Jamieson and Stirling were prepared to invest their own money in setting up a TV station. ...Pickersgill persuaded the cabinet, and Jamieson and Stirling were given the licence. "There were at least a dozen better ways to spend a million dollars of public money for the benefit of Newfoundland," Pickersgill said. "I knew that Geoffrey Stirling and Don Jamieson... were prepared to finance a private television station..." It was the first time the cabinet had overruled a licence recommendation by the CBC board. (Private broadcasters representative Joel) Aldred said the CBC board had been dumb to offer the cabinet a second choice for St. John's.

> One result of this award was the introduction to the world of broadcasting of a singular man who would forever defy convention. Geoff Stirling, a one-time St. John's newspaper publisher, built a broadcast empire in St. John's, Montreal, Windsor, and elsewhere with his audacity, street smarts, and quixotic management style.

"He was absolutely astonishing," says Roger Abbott of the Royal Canadian Air Farce who once worked as an executive at Stirling's Montreal station. "He was rarely in town, and he'd arrive for two or three days and then disappear and we might not see him again for months. But if he didn't like something he'd heard on the air, he'd call up the station and fire the announcer." In those days, Abbott says, Stirling usually wore a t-shirt, jeans and alligator boots, and his curly black hair hung over the collar of his leather jacket.

Nash noted the important role played by Don Jamieson as President of the Canadian Association of Broadcasters, a position which he assumed in 1961 and held for four years. He "brought a new vitality to the group's lobbying and opened a direct avenue into the Liberal party hierarchy. ...No broadcaster .... worked harder and longer for the cause" of private broadcasting. Much of the CAB's lobbying was aimed at forestalling the establishment of new CBC television outlets. The Diefenbaker government between 1957 and 1963 strongly favoured private broadcasting, but there was greater support for the CBC in the Liberal government elected in 1963 under Lester Pearson. The Board of Broadcast Governors, which by then ruled on broadcasting policy, recommended approval of a CBC TV station in St. John's, and the new government accepted this recommendation.

Meanwhile, Nash stated, Don Jamieson as CAB president "made it abundantly clear in speech upon speech across the country that he believed in a minimally regulated private broadcasting system, with the CBC playing a minor, supplementary role as a supplier of cultural programs to private stations. ...he believed broadcasting was primarily for entertainment, not for education, and best done by private enterprise."

MY BRIEF UNION CAREER

In the summer of 1960, less than 10 months after starting to work at CJON, I found myself in the midst of a battle to form a union representing newsroom employees. I was very much in favour of the idea, when it was first broached by local branch organizers from the Canadian Labour Congress. Broadcasting and technical staff at CJON were already unionized and covered under a management agreement with NABET, the National Association of Broadcast Employees and Technicians. Newsroom staff were not included.

This organizing campaign was undertaken by a new entity, called the Newfoundland Journalists and Photographers Union, Local 1593, which had started an unsuccessful bid to unionize news staff at the Evening Telegram. Harold Horwood, then a Telegram columnist and longtime labour union advocate, was a driving force in this endeavour. A little pressure by Horwood and CLC representative Cyril Strong, whom I knew pretty well as a news contact, persuaded me to accept nomination as President of the new Local.

CJON management at that time consisted primarily of co-owner Don Jamieson, his brother, Colin, and a few other top managers. An unseen presence undoubtedly monitoring progress of this bothersome incident was that of the other co-owner, Geoff Stirling. Concentrating in that period on broadcasting holdings in mainland Canada, especially CKGM radio in Montreal, Stirling was seldom seen but his policies were often reflected on the business side of the enterprise. The enigmatic figure of the man behind those perpetual sunglasses showed up at CJON only twice during my six years at the Prince of Wales St. studios.

Our initial efforts to recruit newsmen to join the union were encouraging, sufficiently so that we submitted an application for certification of the local as bargaining agent for newsroom staff. One or two who routinely cozied up to management refused to join, but all others willingly signed up. All very fine, but when the application was presented to CJON management, unimagined pitfalls came to light. All of a sudden, some staff positions we had assumed to be employees were deemed as part of management, while others such as receptionists that we had never thought of as Newsroom-related were designated as inclusions in the purported bargaining group. The numbers that we felt would assure us of a comfortable majority began to crumble. A final blow descended August 22nd (my 30th birthday!) when one of our own, reporter Wally Millman, suddenly handed in his resignation. He did so, he wrote, "for personal reasons", but added this disclaimer: "I wish also to state that I reached this conclusion entirely on my own, and was not in any way tempted to do so by management or anyone connected with the station." This defection did not come as a complete surprise, but it sealed whatever chance we had of winning a representation vote.

Faced with this certainty, the group decided to withdraw the application for certification, and hoped to come back to it on a better day. But that day never came. In a weak attempt to salvage the situation, NABET proposed to open negotiations to have the newsroom employees included in its current agreement with the company. Predictably, this notion too got nowhere.

To be sure, I lived in apprehension for some time afterward on whether my job would survive the experience, but nothing drastic did occur. Relationships within the newsroom cooled noticeably in some instances but time, as always, worked its healing powers to restore eventually much of our former camaraderie.

VOICE REPORTS

One of the interesting innovations in radio news reporting in the early 1960s was the introduction of voice reports for network transmission. Many radio reporters like myself were essentially writers and not announcers, so our voices were seldom heard during newscasts. Given the questionable sound quality and timbre of our voices, this was probably a blessing to the radio audience. Not many of us had been endowed with the resonance and tonal quality of such professional broadcasters as Joel Aldred, Lorne Greene or, for that matter, Don Jamieson.

Yet it was good for the soul, and the ego, to get a chance once in a while to go "on air" with a voice report on some event to which the human voice lent a certain immediacy of impact. Use of taped reports was already in regular use, for example, in reporting on announcements and question period exchanges in the House of Assembly. Also routine was voice reporting from the scenes of a major fire or accident.

Transmission of voice reports beyond our own broadcasting range became possible with the installation of microwave transmission facilities across the province. Canadian Press, the wire services agency serving, and owned by, most of Canada's 100 or so daily newspapers, recognized the special needs and attributes of radio and television news by establishing its Broadcast News Service in 1954. Until BN wire units were installed, local newsrooms had to rely on the Canadian Press wire, which presented news stories in the particular style that newspapers wanted.

When I started in radio, with only a CP wire available, it was often necessary to rewrite CP stories to make them readable on air. Indeed, when I first came to VOCM, where there had been no news staff at all, I found announcers reading CP wire copy stories word for word. The trouble was that they all begin with a certain statement of fact, and add at the end of the sentence "so and so said today." Which sounds extremely silly over the air. One of the first things I did about this was to arrange for a Broadcast News wire machine to be installed, since its copy was written expressly for radio. I also did what I could to rewrite, in radio news style, any wire stories that had a Newfoundland connection.

In the early 60s Broadcast News began urging subscriber stations to feed it voice reports on stories of national interest, so we were always happy to oblige. A periodic voice schedule listing current reports was sent out on the wire, inviting stations to tune in for the next transmission, so they could download the reports they wanted to use.

As a typical example, the BN Voice schedule for 7:30 a.m. July 24, 1961, had nine reports on offer - two from Ottawa, two from West Berlin, one each from London, Tunis, and New Westminster, B.C., and two from Newfoundland:

> Gander, Nfld - (Jack Howlett, CJON) - Yuri Gagarin arrives at Gander, Nfld., en route to Cuba, and St. John's, Nfld - (Nix Wadden, CJON) - Gagarin leaves for Cuba.

Yuri Gagarin was the Soviet Cosmonaut renowned as the first man in space when he successfully completed a single orbit of the earth on April 12, 1961. He was heading for Cuba as part of extensive celebrations in honour of his feat by the communist world. The story had to be really important to warrant CJON sending reporter Jack Howlett to Gander for his brief stopover there.

WRITING NEWS FOR DON JAMIESON

Writing news for broadcast use had its particular requirements, based directly on the characteristics and limitations of these specialized media. Keeping the words short and snappy and readily understandable poses few problems once you get used to it. A lot may depend on how much of a stickler you are for the so-called Queen's English grammar.

Grinding out broadcast news prose probably came easier to me than to many news reporters because I had done precious little newspaper reporting. That stilted, stultifying practice which newspapers used to observe of setting the subject last in lead sentences just didn't work in radio and TV.

Simple straight forward language does apply. And it doesn't have to be strictly grammatical. And certainly does not have to be in proper sentences. Just phrases will do. Once highly sensitive to proper grammar and sentence structure, I learned on the broadcast news jobs to bend the rules slightly for sake of impact and workable communication.

Following such basics of broadcast news proved fully adequate in writing news for Don Jamieson's newscasts. What one had to keep in mind, though, was not to expect one's every written word to be uttered in the news as broadcast. There was one important reality at play here: Don would not read out your words!

Jamieson's nightly News Cavalcade program was not only Newfoundland's most watched and most celebrated television news program. It was also Canada's one and only TV newscast in which the newscaster spoke, but did not read, the news. It was a unique phenomenon to witness at close hand.

The way it worked was that the newsroom staff would write and edit the news of the day in the usual, tried and true manner. Use of film or videotape, whenever available, would be worked into the script at the appropriate phases of the show. The whole paper package would be brought into Don Jamieson's office, well before program time, for him to read in advance.

Don would read it through, and make a few notes for himself, much in the same way as an orator jots down key words to guide him in rehearsing the speech he has in his head to deliver. When satisfied, he would take the sheaf of newscast pages with him, and head for the News Cavalcade set to open the news show. Thence, for the next 30 minutes, the urbane broadcaster's presentation of the news, squarely facing the cameras live, would flow seamlessly with his recounting of the news of the day. But without reading a word of the prepared script. Only occasionally does he bend his eye toward an unseen script, briefly enough to confirm the next news topic, and the eyes turn back steadily toward the camera. The voice never falters, nor wavers, but rolls on in sonorous recitation of the follies, the feats and the fantasies of another day in the life of Newfoundland and Newfoundlanders.

It's an incredible achievement of memory retention, command of language, and sheer facility in regurgitating ideas, expressions and images that reflect the passing parade of local history in the making. The fact that Don could perform this seeming miracle night after night and year after year is what's truly phenomenal - an absolutely unique accomplishment very probably unmatched in the annals of broadcast journalism anywhere in the world.

Perhaps the secret of his success was the sheer volume and variety of Don Jamieson's public speaking experience and of his intimate involvement in the public affairs of Newfoundland. He spoke so frequently and authoritatively on the issues and happenings of the day that an encyclopaedic selection of expressions came readily to mind to meet any current need.

My nearest exposure to his News Cavalcade routine came in reporting on House of Assembly sessions. I was a regular reporter on this beat, and wrote many of the lead stories based on House statements, debates and controversies. On occasion, I brought my report directly to him while he was preparing for the newscast. What impressed me most was the extent to which his broadcast report, while not according word for word with my account, fully captured the gist of the story, and usually included exact quotes I had used in it.

Sometimes, I wrote House reports based not on my own reporting, but on reports done by other staffers and delivered by cab to the station for inclusion in the news. Most often, these reports came in a unique script, the work of Arch Sullivan, another regular legislative staff reporter. Arch - my onetime boss as night editor at the Daily News - was one of a small corps of old school reporters who never learned to type. What he could do to perfection was to record in script form and in clear and accurate detail the essentials of any House business of news interest. The script he used consisted of words set down in single lower case letters such as our grandparents were taught in penmanship classes of long ago. Looking on first glance as a sort of cuneiform markings, the letters spelled out the words as clearly as typeface once you got used to them. I can't remember a single instance where reports based on Arch's unfamiliar markings were ever called into question for accuracy. I kept for years steno notebooks containing my own notes on House debates, along with some of his when he borrowed my notebook. Regrettably, they do not seem to have survived. But I remember them well.

TV INTERVIEWS

Never to be mistaken for a broadcast personality, I nonetheless had to take my turn occasionally at conducting face to face interviews for use on the CJON evening news program. Sometimes, these were pretty short and simple affairs, standing off to one side, off camera, popping questions at the person interviewed. The guest was the only one seen on the screen while all that the viewing audience got from me was the voice over. That kind of thing suited me fine.

On occasion, however, I was tabbed to sit down for a seven minute on-camera interview with some notable who may have wandered in from out of town. With some individuals, this wasn't a tough assignment, since the interviewee was fairly well known and was the type who did not need much prompting to talk confidently into the camera. There were, however, a few TV interviews that have stuck in my mind.

On the down side, there was this chap from Liberia, a tall, lean, taciturn individual who was visiting for some meeting or conference or other, and whom some well meaning person recommended as a good subject for a TV interview. Well, I got together with this gentleman about 15 minutes before the interview, and sought bravely to find out exactly what he had to talk about. What I knew about Liberia before we spoke was negligible, and by the time we were due to begin, was not a lot more. I did know that it was one of those countries where ships could be registered at the drop of a coin, without any nasty regulations to take care of, so I thought we could get into a fine discussion on this absorbing topic. The six or seven minutes I spent in front of that infernal camera, straining to extract answers or comments from Mr. Liberia, were the longest and most excruciating in my life. I don't know if there was any language barrier, but rather think not. He was just one of those people who have very little to say, and especially so when they are staring into a TV camera lens. I will never know how I managed to stretch out this ordeal to fill the requisite seven minutes. One saving grace, however. This interview was done on tape, so there was recourse - the program producer could decide not to use it. And that is probably what he did. I didn't stay around to find out.

My other memorable exposure to TV interviewing involved another individual I knew nothing about, but this time, that wasn't a problem. My guest was a short, stocky, bushy bearded individual ushered into the CJON studio by someone I knew, Harold Horwood. His name, I was told, was Farley Mowat, and he was a writer. There was a real flurry of talk between the two of them as the moments rushed by before show time, so I got hardly a minute to go over what we would be covering in the interview. And then we were on the air - live this time!

So, Mr. Mowat, I began brightly. "I understand you're a writer." And he confirmed that he was. "Well, sir," I said, "what kind of novels to do you write?" There was a pause as Mowat looked at me like I had two heads, and launched into an emphatic dissertation on the distinction between the novels of fiction writers and the kind of books that were his stock in trade. He had by this time published "The Grey Seas Under", recounting the exploits of Foundation Company rescue tugs in the north Atlantic, and several other factual-based works of comparable range and quality. For this interview, I really didn't have to conjure up a succession of clever questions. He was way ahead of me, and proceeded to describe not only his literary achievements but also some of his misadventures sailing along the south coast with Harold Horwood in an accident prone vessel. His written account of these experiences later emerged in his amusing chronicle about "The Boat That Wouldn't Float." Farley was, in short, the ideal interviewee - he loved to talk, and did it very well.

Ironically enough, for all of his fervour in denying that his books were fictional, his superior talents in writing did not gain him universal favour in the science community. Mingling years later with members of that tight knit community, I heard his name uttered more than once as "Hardly Know It." But the man sure can write!

ON THE LIGHTER SIDE

Reporting on local news in the few minutes a broadcast news program usually allows doesn't leave too much time or leeway for waxing poetic, or just plain silly but, sometimes, it just can't be avoided.

The Puffin

Such was my turn of mind one fine day when I was writing and editing a succession of morning (7 am to 9 a.m.) newscasts. It began with a phone call from an excited St. John's resident, reporting an unusual sighting on his property. Quick decision needed - we'd better get Nels, our TV cameraman, and one of our news editors out to the scene pronto. It was done, the camera did its work, and we had a dandy public interest videotape clip to round out that evening's TV news.

But what's the good of a good story if you don't have a bit of fun with it. Something a little special was needed, so this little ditty developed to grace newscasts throughout the day:

> A black and white seabird - I think it's a puffin
> Is on my front lawn - No sir! I'm not bluffin'!
> It must have come here to look for a hideout:
> Say, that's pretty good - My name's Douglas Rideout!
> Well anyway, sir. I'm afraid that he'll die;
> So send someone quick to the street known as Guy.
>
> From this urgent call there was no turning back,
> So the task of removing the bird fell on Jack -
> Who can't tell a puffin apart from an owlet -
> A fact which is strange, since his last name is Howlett!
> But quick as could be with Nels Squires beside him
> (To take this fine picture) he sped out and spied him.
>
> Then, quick as a seagull swoops down on his prey,
> Away whisked the puffin to the shore of the bay;
> Slipped into the water, with one kick and a spin,
> Off paddled the puffin: They watched with a grin;
> Said Rideout: "Thanks be! We made it! Amen!
> There goes one less listener for CJON!"

The Bear

Then there was the time that another strange creature made the news:

"The bear that wasn't there had Thorburn Road residents all agog with excitement last evening. The trouble arose after a lady motorist phoned police that a black bear had lumbered across the road in front of her car. She encountered the animal late yesterday afternoon about a mile past St. Theresa's school. The lady was sure it was a black bear, weighing about 200 pounds.

All night long RCMP were on the watch for the dark intruder. And this morning the quarry was captured. But Fuzzy wuzzy wasn't a bear at all. It was fuzzy all right. And it was black. But it doesn't growl - it barks. The culprit was a friendly, entirely harmless Newfoundland dog, owned by Paddy Whelan of Thorburn Road. Fuzzy wasn't very fuzzy - wuzzy!

The Weather

Even a topic as common as lousy weather, as revealed in this item reported in the Nfld Herald, can inspire the poetic muse on occasion.

The first half of June was made up of the 15 coldest days on record for this month, at least in the St. John's area. Weather records at the St. John's weather station showed that temperatures in the first half of the month were four degrees below normal. Indeed, the weather got so bad that a CJON newsman turned poetic during the week, apparently in an endeavour to shake off the effects of the depressing fog and drizzle. Here's a sample:

> Do you feel you're approaching
> The end of your tether?
> Don't murder your missus,
> It may be the weather!

Are you blue?
Are you jumpy?
Do you feel quite depressed?
Well, move over, my friend,
You're just like the rest.

It's the rain, and the fog,
And the cold, that tells whether
You'll smile, or you'll scream
At your aging grandmother.

So let's all join hands
And sing loud together:
It can't be the climate,
It's only the weather!

11

Farewell to All That

FAREWELL TO ALL THAT

As many people have remarked over the years, journalism is often a good stepping stone to other career pursuits. So I guess they're right because I, like quite a few others of my generation, traded in a dozen or so years of news experience to venture into the realm of government communications. Crossing the great divide, as it were, between the probing, inquisitive craft of questioning the powers that be, to the helpful, cooperative dissemination of answers and explanations from public or private enterprises. Or going over to the dark side, as some would have it.

Enjoyable as the reporting and editing of news had often been, a certain allure existed in the calling of communicators who, when they were good at it, created firm trust and open information exchange with reporters on behalf of their organizations. Professionals of the highest calibre in my experience were such regular news contacts as Leo Shea, public relations director at Pepperrell Air Force Base; Mark Ronayne, Information Officer with the federal Department of Fisheries (DOF) in St. John's and later in Ottawa; Bruce Woodland, Information officer at Tourism and later at DOF; Jim Quigley, also at DOF; and several of the military PR people encountered in the Canadian forces. With all of these individuals, the dominant feeling was one of trust worthiness and dedication to getting the information out, whether it was good news or bad. PR people for the forces, Canadian and American, were products of top notch PR training programs. For the others, news reporting backgrounds fitted them well for understanding reporters' needs, and digging out any answers required.

Jobs in this admirable line of work were not plentiful so, whenever an opening occurred, aspirants from all media outlets were quick to jump into line. I first made the lineup for federal fisheries in 1960 when Bruce Woodland was transferred to B.C. They told me I was one three top candidates, but lost to Jim Quigley who deservedly outranked me with years of excellent service as editor of the Gerald S. Doyle News Bulletin and elsewhere. When he too decided, five years later, to accept a posting to Ottawa with the Federal Department of Forestry and Regional Development, I put in my bid once again. Others I knew who also applied included Charlie Bursey, who had succeeded Jim Quigley at the Doyle Bulletin.

A few days before job interviews were due, Mark Ronayne called me to suggest we go out for a beer together. Then Assistant Director of Information for DOF in Ottawa, he would be sitting in at the selection board convened by the Public Service Commission. Mark and I had known each other since I first began news work, and we usually got together whenever he came to town. When he got around to mentioning the competition, he puzzled me a little by asking how I liked Ottawa. He knew I had visited there a couple of times to attend political conventions. Then he blew me away by suggesting that, if I were interested, I could be considered for a Fisheries information job in Ottawa.

My first reaction was - no way! For a good reason. Little more than six months earlier, Madeline and I had realized a dream by moving into our own house just after Ron, our second child, was born. Moreover, this fine new bungalow on O'Regan Road was only ten minutes away from the Fisheries department offices, then located at the former Pepperrell Air Force Base. The office location was one more reason why I was so keen to get the St. John's Information Officer position. So I really didn't want to think of heading for the mainland.

When my turn came to go before the selection board, I was in for another surprise - a pleasant one in this case, as I knew all of the board members. Least known was the PSC representative, L.R. Scammell, though we had met and talked on the phone several times. Sitting with Mark Royayne was Harold Bradley, Area Manager of the Department of Fisheries, with whom I had often spoken, mostly but not always by phone. The non-fisheries board member was Wes Hutchings, local manager of the Dominion Bureau of Statistics, whom I had often visited in his office and talked to on the phone about population and economic trends.

Results of the board interviews were mixed, I suppose, as I was informed that Charlie Bursey won appointment to the St. John's

Fisheries Information Officer post which I had coveted. However, I was offered the job of Public Information Officer 3 with the Department of Fisheries in Ottawa. After much hesitation, partly to confirm that my moving expenses would be covered by the department, I accepted the offer, and made plans to report for work in Ottawa February 1, 1966. A salary jump of about $1,500 a year did much to dull the pain of emigration!

Looking back more than 40 years to that day, I have no regrets, as this new career worked out very well and, despite occasional setbacks and frustrations, proved highly satisfactory for both work and home life. Ottawa is a beautiful city, even though it's hip deep in bureaucrats.

Nor do I have any misgivings about the dozen or more years I spent labouring in the exciting arena of Newfoundland radio and TV news. Newfoundland is still home in so many ways and certainly in memories of so many family members and good friends, neighbours and co-workers.

Bibliography

Browne, William J., *Eighty-Seven Years A Newfoundlander*. W.J. Browne, St. John's, Nfld., 1984

Camp, Dalton, *Gentlemen, Players and Politicians*. McClelland and Stewart Limited, Toronto 1970

Gwyn, Richard, *Smallwood, The Unlikely Revolutionary*. McClelland and Stewart Limited, Toronto (Revised) 1972

Horwood, Harold, *Among the Lions*. Killick Press, St. John's, Nfld., 2000

Kennedy, Frank, *Flashes From the Past: 42 Years Covering the News*. Breakwater Books, St. John's Nfld, 2000

Kennedy, Frank, *A Corner Boy Remembers: Growing Up in St. John's*. Breakwater Books, St. John's Nfld, 2006

Nash, Knowlton, *The Swashbucklers, The Story of Canada's Battling Broadcasters*, McClelland and Stewart Limited, Toronto, 2001

Stursberg, Peter, *Diefenbaker: Leadership Lost 1962-67*, University of Toronto Press, Toronto, Ont., 1976

Yeo, Leslie, *A Thousand and One First Nights*, Mosaik Press, Oakville, Ont.., 1998

Jamieson, Don, *No Place for Fools, The Political Memoirs of*, Breakwater Books, St. John's, NL, 1989

Blackout
Black crepe shrouds House of Assembly quarters in century old Colonial Building
(Nix Wadden photo)

Winning VOCM 590 crew in 1961 Regatta Press-Radio Race (front l-r): Dick O'Neill, newsroom; Bob Lockhart, announcer; Charlie Noseworthy, operator; (back row): Dave Carter, newsroom; Hall of Fame Coxswain Jack Kenny (father of VOCM staffers Lorraine and Mary); Dave Bastow, operator; Stroke Bob Cole, announcer (courtesy Bob Cole)

Press Club

Press Club 02

EPA St. Pierre
Press and radio representatives mingle with EPA staff to mark St. Pierre inaugural flight: (l-r) - Ewart Young,
Journal of Commerce; Gerry Bowering, Telegram; Ian MacDonald, Canadian Press; Ed Bonnell, Telegram;
Jack Howlett, CJON; Nix Wadden, VOCM; Charlie Bursey, Gerald S. Doyle News Bulletin; Five EPA staff; Noel
Vinnicombe, Daily News; Steve Herder, Telegram; Eric Seymour, Daily News; one EPA staff; Doug Brophy,
CBC; Charles Mardell, CBC (top of steps); EPA staff; Lem Janes, Nfld. Quarterly

Beards
Charlie Noseworthy, Dave Broomfield, Nix Wadden, Ed Flynn, Bill Squires, Hank Harnum, Jim Browne,
Edgar Squires

Ishkov Visit

Media mingling with Russian Minister: (l-r) a Soviet staffer; Gerry Freeman, Canadian Press; Alan Caule, Telegram; A.A. Ishkov; Sylvia Wigh, Telegram; Nix Wadden, Harvey's News; Don Morris, Telegram; Arch Sullivan, Sunday Herald (NW scan)

Knob Lake

Knob Lake visitors include (l-r): Greg O'Grady, Bill Squires, VOCM; Charlie Bursey, Doyle Bulletin; Bill Croke, Telegram; Pat Lees, Daily News; Ian MacDonald. Canadian Press; Darce Fardy, CBC; Harold Morris, CBC (Nix Wadden photo)

PC Convention

(NW scan)

VOCM

Nix Wadden

ABOUT THE AUTHOR

Born and raised in St. John's, Nfld., Nix Wadden was educated at St. Bonaventure's College, attended Memorial University of Newfoundland and completed studies for a B.A. degree at St. Francis Xavier University in Nova Scotia. He got into news work as a part time proofreader at the Daily News, served three years as Harvey's News News Bulletin Editor and founded VOCM's news service in 1957. In 1959, after a brief stint as public relations officer for the Progressive Conservative Party, he joined CJON Radio-TV as senior news editor. He moved to Ottawa in 1966 as an Information Officer, rising to senior communications and public affairs posts in Fisheries and Oceans and Transport departments and the Federal Communications Council. He is married to the former Madeline Roche of St. John's and they have two children, Dianne in Ottawa and Ron in Toronto.

Acknowledgements

I am deeply indebted to family members, friends and colleagues for their kind assistance in this endeavour to recapture the pleasures and the pains of Newfoundland news reporting nearly half a century ago. I particularly want to thank, for sharing their recollections and suggestions, Edsel "Ed" Bonnell, Gerald Bowering, John Carter, Bob Cole, Darce Fardy, Cyril "Cy" Fox, Tom Howley, Frank Kennedy, Bob Lockhart, Ian Macdonald, Dave Maunder, George Perlin, Bill Squires, Sylvia Thomas, Margaret Werthman, and Bruce Woodland. Heather Jamieson helpfully provided information in regard to her late father, Don. Maurice Finn and Bill Callahan, as well as Ed Bonnell and George Perlin, kindly provided valuable contributions to the text.

Special thanks are due to my niece, Marie Wadden, who has given unfailing support and assistance from the beginning, and has contributed a very kind and thoughtful foreword.

I thank Peter and Jean Edwards Stacey of DRC Publishing for their kind support and confidence in making this project possible.

I am grateful for permission granted to use quotations from several valuable sources, particularly Richard Gwyn's Smallwood, the Unlikely Revolutionary, and, courtesy of Dale Russell Fitzpatrick. J.R. Smallwood's I Chose Canada, Other useful information sources, among those noted in the Bibliography, include W.J. Browne's Eighty-Seven Years a Newfoundlander, Frank Kennedy's Flashes From the Past: 42 Years Covering the News, Knowlton Nash's The Swashbucklers, The Story of Canada's Battling Broadcasters, and Don Jamieson's No Place for Fools.

Chris Brookes' excellent radio documentary on Omar Blondahl, The Man Who Sang Goodbye, based on an interview by Neil Rosenberg of Memorial University's Folklore department, shed important light on the latter years of the folk singing broadcaster.

Photo and illustration credits are noted except where their origins could not be ascertained. Unless otherwise indicated, photos are by the author or drawn from personal albums or files.

My greatest regret is the absence of all too many old friends and colleagues in the Newfoundland media who are no longer among us to share in the joys of remembrance of our good old days together.

Finally, heartful gratitude for constant support and timely advice goes out to my dear wife Madeline to whom, along with Dianne, Ron, Lee and Bridget, this book is lovingly dedicated.